Critical praise for the *Undesirable Elements* series

"The cumulative power of these shared stories is nothing short of astonishing. Ping Chong creates a tremendous tapestry of lives."

—TAD SIMONS, *Twin Cities Reader*

"The setup is simple: six black chairs, one white rug and six complete strangers. Ninety minutes later the black chairs and the white rug are still there but the strangers have been replaced by six fascinating, fully formed human beings with whom you have traveled through nine decades and several continents, sharing terror, alienation, disappointment and joy."

—MONICA ENG, *Chicago Tribune*

"An absorbing and sophisticated work."

—MARIANNE EVETT, *Cleveland Plain Dealer*

"This, like any good drama, holds a mirror up to reality, and makes us reflect on our own time, tensions and, even, prejudices as we listen to people who have had to give up so much of their own cultures in order to assimilate into a new one. It's a story we've heard before, but perhaps, not enough."

—TONY CURULLA, *Syracuse Post-Standard*

"The evening is refreshingly low on rhetoric, yet amply pieced with humor, drama, pride and passion. The textured musical layering in *Undesirable Elements* is a captivating metaphor for how cultures dovetail to create the great American social mosaic."

—MISHA BERSON, *Seattle Times*

"It defies cynicism, honoring the magic of resilience and chance."

—CHRISTY DESMITH, *StarTribune*

"Compelling true stories were promised and delivered in *Inside/Out* . . . *voices from the disability community*—as seven people wove their tales into a riveting chronology. Every so often, one performer asked another, 'What does disability mean to you?' The responses were personal and sometimes surprising, and the question compelled viewers to consider for themselves in the wake of the show's coolly shared, sharply rendered lives."

—NELSON PRESSLEY, *Washington Post*

"Chong's elegantly formal staging emphasizes the crafted and selected nature of each story. Six selves are absolutely present, but also distanced by conscious dramatic shaping . . . These harrowing accounts help establish a tacit but telling tension—the piece's dramatic heart, really—between narratives of the past and the theatricality of the present."

—ALISA SOLOMON, *Village Voice*

"It was poetry that filled your heart at one moment and tore it out the next."

—OLLIE REED, JR., *Albuquerque Tribune*

Undesirable Elements

BOOKS BY PING CHONG
AVAILABLE FROM TCG

The East-West Quartet

INCLUDES:

After Sorrow
Chinoiserie
Deshima
Pojagi

Undesirable Elements

INCLUDES:

Undesirable Elements (Original Production, 1992)
Children of War (2002)
UE 92/06 (Anniversary Production, 2006)
Inside/Out . . . voices from the disability community (2008)

Undesirable Elements

Real People, Real Lives, Real Theater

FOUR SELECTED WORKS

Written by Ping Chong, in collaboration with Sara Zatz, Talvin Wilks and the performers

Edited by Sara Zatz

THEATRE COMMUNICATIONS GROUP
NEW YORK
2012

Undesirable Elements is published by Theatre Communications Group, Inc., 520 8th Avenue, 24th Floor, New York, NY 10018–4156

The publication of *Undesirable Elements* by Ping Chong + Company, through TCG's Book Program, is made possible in part by the New York State Council on the Arts with the support of Governor Andrew Cuomo and the New York State Legislature.

TCG books are exclusively distributed to the book trade by Consortium Book Sales and Distribution.

LIBRARY OF CONGRESS CATALOGING-IN-PUBLICATION DATA
Chong, Ping.
Undesirable elements : real people, real lives, real theater : four selected works from the UE series / written by Ping Chong, in collaboration with Sara Zatz, Talvin Wilks and the performers; edited by Sara Zatz.
p. cm.
ISBN 978-1-55936-397-6
I. Zatz, Sara. II. Wilks, Talvin. III. Title.
PS3553.H586U53   2012
812'.54—dc23   2012006379

Cover design by Mark Melnick
Cover photographs: (front, top) Adam Nadel; (front, bottom) Earl Richardson Photography; (back) Chris Hartlove
Book design and composition by Lisa Govan

First Edition, October 2012

Special Thanks

Bruce Allardice, Victoria Abrash, John Bernstein, Tim Bond, Claudine Brown, Rohit Burman, Ben Cameron, Elizabeth Elliott, Dr. Ahmed Ferhadi, Ellis Finger, Brandon Fradd, Angel Gardner, Global Kids, Courtney Golden, Taryn Higashi, Steven Hitt, Jane Jung, Susan Kennedy, Roberta de Martini, Nakissa Modir, Leyla Modirzadeh, Adam Nadel, Jesca Prudencio, Michael Rohd, Carlos Gutierrez-Solana, Ellen Stewart, Hiroshi Takahagi, Watoku Ueno, VSA, Philippa Wehle, Micki Wesson, Talvin Wilks, Sachiko Willis, and especially Anna, Cochise, Eva, Hiromi, Olga, Tania, Trinket, and all the hundreds and hundreds of "undesirables" who have shared their stories with us over the years.

Ping Chong + Company would like to acknowledge the National Endowment for the Arts, The Nathan Cummings Foundation, Doris Duke Charitable Foundation, and MetLife Foundation for their support of the *Undesirable Elements* series over the years.

Contents

Introduction

By Alisa Solomon

I t's hard to pinpoint when, exactly, the phrase "undesirable elements"
entered the human lexicon, but the tendency of dominant groups
to draw borders around their power seems as old as history itself. In
American usage, at least (after conceptual appearances that go at
least as far back as the Bible and ancient Greek drama), the term
begins to perform its fence-building function in the late 1800s in
the context of immigration debates. A Congressional report from
1877, for example, warns:

> An indigestible mass in the community, distinct in lang-
> uage, pagan in religion, inferior in mental and moral
> qualities, and all peculiarities, is an undesirable element in
> a republic, but becomes especially so if political power is
> placed in its hands . . . the laws should discourage the large
> influx of any class of population to whom the ballot cannot
> be safely confided.

The report was prepared by a joint committee of Congress charged
with investigating the impact of Chinese immigrants, who had been
streaming into the U.S. for some thirty years at that point—first,
pulled by the California Gold Rush and, then, recruited as laborers
for the Transcontinental Railroad. Nearly 125,000 Chinese were
recorded as arriving in the 1870s alone.

Though the report paved the way for the Chinese Exclusion Act of 1882, it wasn't only Chinese newcomers who were regarded as likely to poison the stew in America's melting pot. "Lunatics, idiots and persons likely to be a public charge" were also named in the legislation. And later policies targeted Italians and Eastern European Jews. Indeed, the history of immigration laws from the 1870s until 1924 (when a draconian quota system was installed to choke off the flow of "undesirables") reads like an ever-swelling list of the inadmissible. Over the years, "feeble-minded persons," epileptics, anarchists, paupers, Japanese laborers and, among others, people without enough cash for the steadily increasing entry-port fees, joined the roster of those to be turned away from American shores. Newspaper stories, meanwhile, freely applied the label "undesirable element" to a wide range of immigrants. In an early usage, for example, a *New York Times* report on the St. Patrick's Day Parade of 1872, noted that "for the Irishman," most Americans "have an undoubted liking. It is only when his unquiet character is complicated with whiskey, religious fanaticism and barroom politics that he becomes an undesirable element of the community."

The phrase was no mere metaphor: the clamorous movement agitating for restrictive immigration policy regarded the "unfit" as possessing—as one of their leaders put it—"defective and degenerate protoplasm." It was as if "undesirables" literally carried a toxic substance within their own bodies that threatened to contaminate the body politic.

Ping Chong's invoking and upending of this shameful phrase is no mere metaphor, either. Theater, after all, puts live bodies before us, and in Chong's extraordinary series of choral documentary dramas, bodies that had once been rendered "undesirable elements" become—as bodies on stage always do, through the theater's magical mechanisms of empathy and display—emphatically desirable.

That's not all. The performers—who are not professional actors—live in the community where they are performing and, most important, they are telling their own stories. Through the act of naming themselves and recounting how they came to be here—quite literally here, now, in the theater, as well as here in this town in the United States—they claim their place in the body politic. Theater, like America, is a space of self-making. The *Undesirable Elements* series offers a distilled, elegant demonstration of that exhilarating and complicated process.

The scripts collected in this volume represent only four key stops on a zig-zagging, ongoing journey that Chong has been making with these plays for twenty years. At this writing, more than forty versions have been created in such cities as Atlanta, Chicago, Cleveland, Minneapolis, Long Beach, Newark and Seattle, and new editions are on the horizon for years to come. (There have also been productions overseas, for example, in Berlin, Rotterdam and Tokyo.) Typically, participants in each production share the experience of having been born in one culture and, by force or choice or a messy combination of the two, having ended up in another. Increasingly in recent years, though, a production is shaped around a more specific common experience: For example, *Children of War* presents young people who endured violence in their home countries before coming to the U.S. as refugees; *Native Voices—Secret History* reveals stories of local Native Americans in Lawrence, Kansas; *Inside/Out* centers on people with disabilities; *Secret Survivors* on the experiences of survivors of child sexual abuse. *Women of the Hill*, brings together a multigenerational group of women from Pittsburgh's famous African-American neighborhood, the Hill District. Among hundreds, *Undesirable Elements* participants have included a gay Vietnamese man who grew up in Texas, a Chickasaw Native American whose parents were forcibly settled in Los Angeles, a Tongan American who was raised Mormon in Utah, a man with Moebius syndrome who wandered accidentally into a theater group and was transformed by the experience of choosing to let people stare at him on stage, a Ukrainian who waited in postwar DP camps as a child before being approved for entrance to the U.S. In one sense or another, all the participants in *Undesirable Elements* have been displaced persons.

The project remains durable and portable for two interconnected reasons: The scaffolding that all versions of *Undesirable Elements* share is as firm and flexible as bamboo. (Chong's collaborator, Sara Zatz, likens it to a sonnet, whose structure stays solid as the contents shift.) And the narratives it supports are as rich and abundant as the earth's minerals—if, like Chong, one knows how to locate them, bring them to the surface, and make them shine. He finds them by partnering with local host organizations—YMCAs, universities, theater groups, social service agencies—and talking to people interested in taking part. From some twenty-five interviewees, Chong and his artistic collaborators cast five, six or seven, and then question them at greater length, spending several hours with each. From their answers, Chong creates the script. He crosscuts their birth stories, anecdotes, memories and ideas to create a chronology, and slots them into his frame, like tongues into a groove. Over a period of about six months, Ping Chong + Company works with the group in several stints of a few weeks each, polishing the script, rehearsing and then performing.

The project began in 1992, when Chong was invited by Artists Space in New York to make an installation called "A Facility for the Channeling and Containment of Undesirable Elements," and then asked to make a performance piece to go with it. At the time, Chong recalled an experience of working in English with multilingual artists, who had switched into other languages during breaks. Struck by the ease and comfort of the group's collaboration, despite the fact that they had come from different cultures, he decided to supply the requested performance piece by calling together a set of performers who spoke several languages and had not been born in New York, and by asking them about their lives. Serendipitously and swiftly, *Undesirable Elements* took shape.

But in many ways, Chong had been preparing for it for years. For more than two decades he'd been creating graceful, imagistic, multimedia theater pieces in New York's experimental theater scene and, just as important, he'd been wrestling artistically with the experience of being an outsider for his entire creative life. Chong's parents, performers in the Chinese opera, had arrived in North America on a theatrical tour and decided to stay. Chong was born in Toronto in 1946 (three years after the U.S. repealed the Chinese Exclusion Act) and shortly thereafter, the family moved to New York's Chinatown. Until he went to junior high with kids from the immigrant Italian community nearby, everyone around Chong spoke Cantonese (his parents spoke no English). Chong likely wasn't familiar with the phrase "undesirable element" as a boy, but he learned what it felt like. He smacked into the concept's walls the minute he ventured north of Canal Street for high school. As an applicant to a school specializing in the arts, he was declared inept for not knowing the paintings of Titian, but as Chong made his way into the art world nonetheless (studying film and graphic design at the School of Visual Arts and Pratt Institute), he quickly learned that being an outsider, difficult as it was at times, afforded him a kind of double vision that was valuable to him as an artist. "As a young adult, I felt like I was sitting on a fence staring at two cultures," he wrote in 1988 in an introduction to the published text of his 1981 performance piece *Nuit Blanche: A Select View of Earthlings.* "You go out into the bigger world and start looking at it with the kind of objectivity an anthropologist has."

It's hard to generalize about Chong's work over the years (he has produced dozens of performances and installations that have employed video, film, sound recordings, choreography, historical texts and/or various kinds of puppets, among other media and material), but if there's a single thread running through his career thus far, it unwinds from the young man on that fence. Many of Chong's pieces (beginning with his first independent work, *Lazarus* [1972], whose protagonist was isolated behind a mummy-like head wrapping) center on characters who are somehow shut out or estranged from the world around them. In a memorable scene from *Rainer and the Knife* (1981), a boy on whom a murder will be pinned, watches remotely as society marches by in regimented steps. *Kind Ness* (1986) was set in "Suburbia, USA" of the 1950s and 1960s and followed an adolescent newcomer—alien in his hairy gorilla head—as he assimilates into the new culture and loses touch with his origins. Later works, chiefly a concentrated quartet made in the 1990s, comprising *Deshima, Chinoiserie, After Sorrow* and *Pojagi,* explore misperceptions and historical tensions between East and West. Such themes course through the bloodstream of *Undesirable Elements* as well, though the multi-autobiographical storytelling at the heart of the series came as a surprising development in Chong's repertoire. Until this project, Chong's work, varied as it was, spoke in a single—and singular—voice. Though he might have tapped different parts of his register or struck varying tones, he (properly and agreeably) held the floor. *Undesirable Elements,* however, is a choral work in which each participant chimes in equally. Chong's aesthetic and worldview provide the framework, but the stories—their events, imagery, and emotions—do not stem from him. He makes a lovely structure by virtue of which those stories can be told together, and then he gently steps out of the way. Opening the space to multiple tales, viewpoints and sentiments about migration is probably what catalyzed the expansion of the series' scope: Once Chong shared the platform with diverse takes on an experience similar to his own as an outsider from an immigrant family, it was not a huge step to share it with people whose specific experiences—as war refugees, abuse survivors or people with disabilities, for example—may have differed from his, but that landed them within the same structure of feeling. They, too, had been rendered "undesirable." Like any true artistic leap, Chong's plunge into *Undesirable Elements* seemed both overdetermined and like a departure.

That's true in formal terms, too. *Undesirable Elements* shares the spare elegance that has distinguished Chong's pieces from the beginning—striking images made of simple means and staged beautifully with little fanfare—but puts it to new uses. In the *Undesirable*

Elements productions, the actors sit in a semi-circle on black chairs, a half-moon floor covered with crystalline rock salt spreading out in front of them, a lunar orb glowing on the wall or curtain behind. When they enter at the production's start, they stand briefly and still in front of their chairs, each in her or his own pool of light. Stark and pretty, this isolation soon dissolves and the cast members create commonality as they move in unison (in early versions of the series, at least) through a set of stylized gestures: arms stretched out in front, then crossed at the chest, then dropped to the sides. They offer greetings in their first languages, then, in turn, give (and explain) their names and the circumstances of their birth. And soon they are telling their tales, sometimes adding song, folklore or poetry in their native tongues.

Coming from vastly different places, backgrounds and age groups, the performers quickly emerge as distinct individuals, and yet they flow in and out of each other's narratives in ways that bind them into a collectivity. It's not just the ritualized choreographic movement—which also includes some punctuating hand-clapping—that achieves this coherence; it's also the division of lines. First, the performers do not sequentially tell unbroken personal accounts of their lives; Chong has torn apart what might conventionally have been a series of monologues and rewoven them into a complex narrative of intertwining strands. Then he's threaded in historical events that not only form the backdrops of the performers' lives, but set their destinies in motion. For instance, one repeated trope goes: "If it had not been for _____ , I would not be here now." The blank is filled by astonishing incidents: a father's last-minute decision during World War II to go study in Osaka instead of Hiroshima; a performer's unconscious choice to use one bathroom in her family's Beirut home in 1975, moments before a bomb blasted into the other one. Individual stories are also framed by world events in march-of-time announcements: "1989, November 9. The Berlin Wall falls." "1990. After eleven years of war, there are free elections in Nicaragua." "1991. Syria and the U.S. forces are no longer in Lebanon." The productions proceed chronologically, each participant describing her or his own journey, in terms both epic (amid wars, colonial rule, economic deprivation, bigotry) and intimate (the astounding first bite into a crisp apple, the severing of ties with family).

But the performers do not tell their stories alone. Sometimes the entire company picks up a phrase of one person's chronicle to recite chorally. Sometimes a performer takes the part of a character in another's story, or even speaks in another character's first-person voice. Now and then, Chong even has the performers change seats.

All this contextual scene-setting, slicing and dicing and doling out of lines, and speaking in the other's voice, generates *Undesirable Elements'* greatest power: It shows people engaging life as subjects in history. This is a huge achievement in our hyper-confessional culture, when therapized self-revelation drives the worst of autobiographical performance art and personal gut-spilling splatters across the networks and cable channels on daytime TV. (The formality of the staging, along with the performers' use of scripts, which are perched on black music stands in front of each chair, also helps to steer the work away from melodrama and sentimentality: It signals that we are not watching a sensationalistic gush of self-exposure, but a carefully crafted drama.) Thus *Undesirable Elements* joins a great American tradition that includes such works as James Agee and Walker Evans's *Let Us Now Praise Famous Men*; Anna Deavere Smith's interview-based plays, which she collectively terms "A Search for the American Character"; Studs Terkel's monumental oral histories; and National Public Radio's "StoryCorps" project—artful efforts to document our country through its myriad voices and, like Whitman, to let us hear them singing.

As with these other complex works, America is a complex place in *Undesirable Elements*. The series—especially the productions that focus on immigrants to the U.S.—run the risk of presenting a straight progress narrative in which the U.S. simply embraces its newcomers, sheltering them from violence, corruption, poverty or whatever else constrained their lives elsewhere. Sometimes the series does, but that's never the whole story: Even those who have fled mayhem and savagery (a participant in *Children of War* recounts how she raced through Sierra Leone's corpse-strewn streets) still miss the sounds and scents of home.

To this day, such longing and the attendant efforts to keep the languages, cuisines, folkways and cultures from that erstwhile home alive in this country—indeed, to make them *at* home in this country—are confronted by the xenophobia that, like a dog in chase, always runs barking after America's welcoming impulses. Lately, it has been biting: Arizona's draconian 2010 law against undocumented migrants is seeing copycat measures around the country. And the racist rhetoric that enables and is enflamed by calls for harsh restrictions rings with the disgraceful old echoes. As recently as 2007, an amendment to a Utah Republican Party platform plank advised:

... the immigrant who cannot be adjusted with a reasonable degree of readiness to the customs and institutions of his adopted country brings an undesirable element into the community and would better be excluded.

The *Undesirable Elements* productions, dancing on that tension, easily stamp out such bigoted sentiments. They present Americans who are neither to be despised and feared nor to be superficially celebrated. But to be attended to, recognized and heard.

New York City
March 2012

ALISA SOLOMON is a teacher, writer, and dramaturg. She directs the Arts & Culture MA program at Columbia University's Graduate School of Journalism.

Undesirable Elements

Notes on Production

A NOTE ON THE USE OF LANGUAGE

Undesirable Elements was originally conceived around the idea of the sound of multiple languages at play, and Ping Chong sought out participants who spoke multiple languages for this purpose. In many versions, cast members introduce themselves in the language of their birth at the top of the production, and then reintroduce themselves in English at the end. This structure intentionally creates an initial feeling of distance and alienation in the audience, and then a subsequent sense of recognition and familiarity, after life stories have been revealed, and identities claimed onstage.

In productions that focus on issues of cultural identity, performers often recite a poem or sing a song in their traditional language. Again, these sections are deliberately not translated, and are instead used as transitions in the narrative, and an aural respite from the march of personal history. These moments are lyrical, haunting and mysterious for the audience (unless they happen to speak the same language as a performer, in which case it becomes a moment of secret understanding).

For this volume, songs and poems have been noted in the stage directions, but not printed. Original languages and alphabets are used in the introductory sections without translation, to replicate the experience in the theater. Elsewhere in the scripts, lines are printed in either the original language, for longer phrases, or in transliteration when the English translation is repeated immediately after, for shorter phrases.

A NOTE ON STAGING

All *Undesirable Elements* productions use the same basic production concept, with artistic variations incorporated into specific productions. The scenic elements consist of music stands, chairs and microphones for the performers, arranged around a semicircular "half-moon" of white rock salt or a white painted floor. Each chair is situated in a "pool" of light, which can highlight individual speakers or the entire cast of performers. Additional lighting includes atmospheric color washes on the floor and on the cyc, as well as a blue circular "moon" of light focused above the performers on a cyc or projection screen. The early performances used projection sequences of outlines of unidentified countries within an enclosed circle. Each country appeared the same size within the circle, regardless of actual geographic scale (i.e., China appeared to be the same size as Sri Lanka). As the production themes have evolved beyond national/cultural identities, some productions now include more elaborate projection sequences that incorporate personal imagery from cast members, historic maps and archival images from local communities.

Undesirable Elements productions are spare, elegant and primarily static. Once the performers enter the space, they do not leave until the conclusion of the show. With the exception of the occasional orchestrated seat change, or moment of dance shared by a performer, the true sense of movement in the production comes not from physical movement, but from the rapid aural movement of the language and dialogue of the script itself. For this reason, Ping Chong describes *Undesirable Elements* as "a seated opera for the spoken word."

Embedded within the script are sequences of claps that provide punctuation, rhythm and momentum to the spoken dialogue, as well as adding emphasis to key moments. When the stage directions indicate "all clap," the cast is clapping one time, sharply, in unison. In other instances, the cast may clap two, five or ten times, as indicated in the stage directions. These longer clap sequences typically serve as transitional moments into and out of seat changes, sequences of songs or poems, or to demarcate the beginning and ending of distinct sections within the show.

Undesirable Elements
(Original Production)

New York City / 1992

Conceived, written and directed by Ping Chong

IN COLLABORATION WITH:
M. Cochise Anderson
Eva Gasteazoro
Emerald Trinket Monsod
Hiromi Sakamoto
Tania Salmen
Regine Anna Seckinger
Olga Kyrychenko Shuhan

In 1992, Carlos Gutierrez-Solana, then director of Artists Space in Manhattan, asked me to create a visual arts installation titled *A Facility for the Channeling and Containment of Undesirable Elements*. A few weeks before the opening, he asked me to make a performance piece to go with it. I had just returned from teaching a ten-day workshop in Amsterdam, with young students from all over the world. The one requirement for the workshop was that the participants speak English. We worked, ate and played together for ten days. In the evenings, we would sit in one of the many charming "brown" or "white" bars in Amsterdam and talk about everything from food to politics to sex. During one of these evenings it suddenly struck me that I had been hearing all these different languages and English flying back and forth across the table, and I thought: Here we are, a group of people from all over the world, from different cultures and experiences, engaged in a constructive and collective endeavor—the exploration of artistic expression. We were not shouting at each other nor killing each other. We were learning about each other. I wondered that night whether it was possible to make a work using multiple languages, testifying to the history of lives lived and the phenomena of culture itself. I stored this thought in the back of my mind, not knowing that opportunity would arrive in the form of Carlos Gutierrez-Solana a few weeks later. So I set to work on what would become the first *Undesirable Elements*, which was performed in the installation itself at Artists Space. My approach wasn't scientific. I asked friends to introduce me to bilingual people and one person led to another. I had no idea at the time that that production would lead to nearly fifty original works over the next twenty years, in communities around the country and the world. *Undesirable Elements* has taken me to places—geographic, psychic and spiritual—that I never imagined, and it continues to inspire me.
—*Ping Chong*

PRODUCTION HISTORY

The first production of the *Undesirable Elements* series premiered at Artists Space in New York on October 22, 1992, as part of a visual arts installation by Ping Chong entitled "A Facility for the Channeling and Containment of Undesirable Elements." It was conceived and directed by Ping Chong. It was written by Ping Chong in collaboration with the cast. The sound designer was Brian Hallas, the lighting designer was Tom Hase, and the lighting operator was Nancy Kramer. The assistant director was Regine Anna Seckinger and the managing director was Bruce Allardice. The performers were M. Cochise Anderson, Eva Gasteazoro, Emerald Trinket Monsod, Hiromi Sakamoto, Tania Salmen, Regine Anna Seckinger and Olga Kyrychenko Shuhan.

Seven stools are arranged in a gallery space. Throughout the space are recessed pools of thick black and ochre liquid, six feet in diameter, which are lit to glow. The floor around the pools is covered in salt crystals. The stools are placed in the salt. The ensemble sits on the stools and reads from their scripts throughout the performance. None of the performers ever leaves the stage. The audience watches the performance seated on the catwalks along the gallery space.

Sound: a haunting Norwegian incantation fades in. Lights slowly come up. One at a time, the performers enter and stand at their stools, where they face each other. As the incantation plays, the performers face the audience and slowly, ritually, raise their arms to the side, then bring them forward, crossing them in front of their bodies, then open them out again, and bring them down to their sides. This motion is repeated slowly and gracefully in unison, as if they are moving through water. The incantation fades out at the end of the gestures.

COCHISE: *Tonshpah, Kaleah.*
TANIA: يلا بلشنا
HIROMI: さあ、始めましょう.
TRINKET: *Simulan natin.*
ANNA: *Lasst uns anfangen.*
OLGA: Починаймо!
EVA: *Comencemos de una vez.*
COCHISE *(Translating for all)*: Let's get started.

(The ensemble sits on their stools.)

TANIA: سلمان، بيروت، لبنان. يوم المليت. ألف وتسعمية وتلاتة وستين. سبت تماني عشية. حصان اسمه تانيا ربح السباق هاليوم.

OLGA: Мене звуть Оля Кириченко. Я народилася в місті Києві, в Україні, дев'ятого листопада тридцять сьомого року о п'ятій годині по полудні. Був полум'яний захід сонця.

TRINKET: *Trinket Monsod. Quezon City, Philippines. Labing anim ng Nobembre, isang libo, siyam na raan limamput lima. Alas nueve ng umaga. E. Emerald para sa aking ina, Estrella. T. Trinket para sa aking ama, Tomas.*

EVA: *María Eva Gasteazoro Rivas, nacida de parto provocado en Chinandega, Nicaragua. El 12 de diciembre de 1952 a las 11:30 de la noche.*

ANNA: *Regine Anna Seckinger. Freiburg, Baden. Germany. 7 Juli 1967. 14 Uhr 32. Sankt Joséphskrankenhaus. In einem Gewitter.*

HIROMI: 阪本洋三。昭和36年９月３日、台風の晩に生まれました。大阪府堺市出身の日本人です。

COCHISE: *Cochise Anderson. Sa holth chifo ut, Cochise Anderson. Sa utta chuli pokoli tukla awa chukale hunalitulhapi. Los Angeles, California, U.S.A. Iklunne anockaka engh iklunne anockaka tohme pulli.*

(All clap.)

TANIA: *Kariff.* Autumn.

OLGA: *Osin'.* Autumn.

TRINKET: *Katapusan ng panahon ng pag-ulan.* The rainy season has ended.

EVA: *Había dejado de llover.* The rainy season had ended.

ANNA: *Sommer.* Summer.

HIROMI: *Banka, shoshu.* Late summer, beginning of fall.

COCHISE: *Tohme-pulli.* Summer.

(All clap.)

HIROMI: Oji-san, Oba-san, Koi-san, Goshujin, Aneki, Oniisan, Oba-san, Okusan Goshujin.

TRINKET: In Japanese—in his language, in Hiromi's language—unless you are a really close friend, you would not call him by his first name. You would use his last name and add *san*—*Sakamoto-san*. This is a very convenient word. It can mean Mr., Mrs., Sir, etcetera. The other way of addressing someone is to use the person's social title or position. For example, your neighbor's wife would be Mrs. Housewife: *Oku-san*; your boss would be Mr. Boss: *Bucho*. In the higher positions, *san* is not used, because higher positions have the connotation of politeness already built in. There are also ways of naming people by their professions, as in *Tofuya-san* for the tofu vendor and *Sakana-san* for the fish seller.

HIROMI: In Japan, my parents are the only people who would call me by my first name. Hiromi. Hiromi. Hiromi.

(All clap.)

TRINKET: The Philippines.

(The following section is performed in a call and response between Trinket and the ensemble.)

TRINKET:	ALL:	TRINKET:	ALL:
Epiphania	Name	Paning	Nickname
Toribia	Name	Bibing	Nickname
Teofilo	Name	Pilo	Nickname
Napoleon	Name	Fuji	Nickname
Katherine	Name	Girlie	Nickname
Fernando	Name	Nanding	Nickname
Fernando II	Name	Don	Nickname
Fernando III	Name	Chito	Nickname
Abner Xavier	Name	Butch	Nickname
Fidelis	Name	Bongbong	Nickname
Fe Eloisa	Name	Loly	Nickname
Robert	Name	Jumbo	Nickname
Arthur	Name	Tiny	Nickname
Estrella	Name	Yeng, Tilyeng, Gypsy	Nickname
Trinket	Name	Inkai, Inket	Nickname

(Everyone changes seats and sits down, except Anna, who remains standing.)

ANNA: Regine Anna Seckinger. *Mutter.*
COCHISE: Mother.
ANNA: Herta Irma Seckinger. *Vater.*

13

COCHISE: Father.

ANNA: Karl Friedrich Seckinger. *Chemiker.*

COCHISE: Chemist.

ANNA: *Grossmütter.*

OLGA: Grandmothers.

ANNA: Anna Maria Schwald. Karola Steingräber. *Grossväter.*

OLGA: Grandfathers.

ANNA: Otto Schwald. *Maschinenmeister.*

OLGA: Machinist

ANNA: Karl Seckinger.

OLGA: Orphan.

ANNA: *Urgrossmütter.*

HIROMI: Great-grandmothers.

ANNA: Emma Becherer. Maria Schwald. *Urgrossväter.*

HIROMI: Great-grandfathers.

ANNA: August Becherer. *Mechaniker.*

HIROMI: Mechanic.

ANNA: Gustav Otto Schwald. *Maschinenmeister.*

HIROMI: Machinist.

ANNA: *Ur-Urgrossmütter.*

TRINKET: Great-great-grandmothers.

ANNA: Katharina Becherer. Barbara Lenz. Maria Katharina Schwald.
    Maria Elisabetha Oswald. *Ur-Urgrossväter.*

TRINKET: Great-great-grandfathers.

ANNA: Johannes Baptist Becherer. *Gastwirt.*

TRINKET: Pub owner.

ANNA: Johann Jakob Lenz. *Weichenwärter.*

TRINKET: Switchman. Undesirable element. Discontinued profession.

ANNA: Karl Friedrich Oswald. *Dreher.*

TRINKET: Woodturner.

ANNA: Gustav Schwald. *Nagelschmied.*

TRINKET: Nailmaker.

ALL: Undesirable element. Discontinued profession.

(Eva rings bell. The ensemble changes places while reciting vendor calls from their native language. Eva stops ringing the bell. Silence. Everyone sits on their stools.)

EVA: Don José Agustín de Gasteazoro y Urquiza, married to Doña María Teresa Téllez y Venerio, arrived in Nicaragua in 1775. They were my great-great-great-grandparents. As a legacy from the King of Spain, they received eighteen thousand heads of cattle, one hundred horses, two ceremonial carriages, twenty oxcarts and thirty thousand hectares, including one hundred Indians and a volcano. Don José Gasteazoro y Robelo, my great-grandfather, had to possess every virgin living in his domain. One rainy night, he gambled away the entire property. Don José del Carmen Gasteazoro y Montealegre, a doctor, and a man of many languages—my grandfather—recovered the land, the horses and the cattle. It was rumored that he would climb the volcano at night and return the following morning with saddle-bags filled with gold. For every Indian who died on his land, a new calf would be born. People said he had sold his soul to the devil.

(All clap.)

1926.

ALL: 1926.

EVA: Because of political unrest in the country, the U.S. sends marine forces to Nicaragua to protect American interests. They remain there until 1933.

(All clap.)

OLGA: 1941.

ALL: 1941.

OLGA: German forces occupy Kiev. My first vivid memory is consoling my mother and begging her to stop crying when we were hiding under our house during an air raid. The next four years of my life are full of war memories, like running into the woods or into the fields, or hiding in cellars from bomb explosions.

(All clap.)

1943.

ALL: 1943.

OLGA: My parents decide to escape from Ukraine and the terrors of Stalin's communism. It was a slow and dangerous flight to the West through war-torn countries of Poland, Czechoslovakia and, finally, Germany where my father and teenage brother had to work in German labor camps.

(All clap.)

ANNA: 1944.

ALL: 1944.

ANNA: January 12. Gertrude Seele, a German resistance fighter, is captured by the Nazis. She writes a letter to her seven-year-old daughter. (*She reads the letter aloud:*)

My Dear, Dear Little Daughter:

Today your mother has to die. I think of you and my heart is breaking. Be good to your grandparents and make them—and me—proud by growing up to be a sincere, honest and courageous person. Farewell, my lovely little daughter—in my thoughts, I embrace and I kiss you one last time.

All my love,

Your Mother

(*All clap.*)

OLGA: 1945.

ALL: 1945.

OLGA: Now, the threat of bombs has been replaced by the threat of repatriation. Immediately after the war, many people were sent back to their homeland, usually against their will. Even those who were taken by Germans as labor force or POWs preferred to remain rather than return to certain punishment, such as Siberian labor camps or maybe execution. Stalin felt that anyone who had been to the West, for whatever reason, was corrupt and an enemy of the people. These were frightening times. Some would even commit suicide rather than face repatriation. The next seven years of my life were spent in one DP—or displaced persons—camp, or another. As people were immigrating to various parts of the world, smaller camps would close and we had to keep moving.

(*All clap.*)

HIROMI: 1945.

ALL: 1945.

HIROMI: In 1945, my father was accepted by two universities. World War II was at its peak, all the people were supposed to be the children of the godlike Emperor Hirohito and most Japanese really believed it. In those days, if you were good at science or mathematics, you were allowed to do research in military-related industries. But if you wanted to major in humanities, such as literature or linguistics, you had to go and fight in the front lines of the war—even before you were fifteen. My father was accepted by Hiroshima University in the spring of 1945. It was his dream to study literature there, but, instead, he majored in science and math at a university in Osaka. Half a year later, Hiroshima was attacked by the infamous bomb and the war ended. If he had gone to Hiroshima University, I would not be here now.

(All clap.)

ANNA: 1945
ALL: 1945.
ANNA: My grandmother slaughters the last of her chickens.

(All clap.)

TRINKET: 1945.
ALL: 1945.
TRINKET: February 3. Manila, Philippines. The U.S. ends three years of Japanese occupation and over three centuries of Spanish rule. A year later, on July 4, the U.S. grants Filipinos independence, but only after its leaders sign a military agreement and the Bell Trade Act, which makes the dollar the master of the Filipino soul. *(Singing)* "This way, this way, this way down, down to a Filipino . . ."

(All clap.)

TANIA: 1945.
ALL: 1945.
TANIA (*In Arabic*): ألف وتسعمية وخمسة وأربعين، جدي بيبعت بيي من بيروت لفنزويلا، ليشتغل ويعمل مصاري.
(Translating) My grandfather sends my father from Beirut to Venezuela to make his fortune.

(All clap.)

COCHISE: 1945.
ALL: 1945.
COCHISE: My father looks up into the sky and sees a red-tailed hawk. He is two years old.

(All clap.)

OLGA: 1949.

ALL: 1949.

OLGA: My mother dies after a long illness.

(All clap.)

1952.

ALL: 1952.

OLGA: February. We are finally allowed to immigrate to the United States, crossing the Atlantic on the last navy ship that carried war refugees from Germany. After twelve stormy days, one misty morning, we slowly moved into New York Harbor and, as if in a dream, through the fog, I saw the long awaited Statue of Liberty and the magnificent Manhattan skyline. To this day, that was the most exciting sight of my life.

(All clap.)

COCHISE: 1952.

ALL: 1952.

COCHISE: By 1952, the U.S. policy regarding relocation and termination of all Native American tribes was in full swing. Grandma and Grandpa were given one-way tickets to Los Angeles so they could eventually achieve the American dream. They never did.

(All clap.

One by one, each performer sings a song in his/her native language in the following order: Tania, Trinket, Hiromi, Anna, Eva, Cochise, Olga. These songs are not translated, but create a medley of different languages and sounds.)

EVA: What do you think of when I say the word "Nicaragua"?

COCHISE: A con man named Walker.

TANIA: My pen pals in high school.

ANNA: Rice and beans.

HIROMI: Politically unstable.

COCHISE: Hot.

TRINKET: Sandinistas.

OLGA: Earthquakes.

EVA: I think of the old family house and the *buganvilias* there.

TANIA: Anna, what do you think of when I say the word "Germany"?

ANNA: Nietzsche, even though I don't know much about him. Rhubarb. The past. Walnuts on freshly baked and buttered bread. The inevitability of history's impact. *Gedächtniskirche.* Mushroom hunting. White sausages, black sausages, long sausages, short sausages—sausages. A wall and no wall. Guilt for a reason and for no reason at all. My first kiss. The White Rose. A slice of Linzer torte. Collective unconscious.

TRINKET: What do you think of when I say the word "Philippines"?

COCHISE: A lot of tiny little islands. Beautiful women. Political extremes. Aquino's assassination. Americanization. Shoes, shoes, shoes.

OLGA: Cochise, what do you think of when I say the words "Native American"?

COCHISE: We're still here. *Iposeh.* Grandma. Sterilization of women. Children being adopted by white families. Alcohol. Infighting. Indian fry bread. "Do you live on a reservation?" "You're the first Indian I've ever met!" "Okla-Houma." BIA: Bureau of Indian Affairs—slash—Bully Indians Around. Why is there a Bureau of Indian Affairs? Why don't we have a Bureau of Irish Affairs? Redskin. Tanto. Squanto. Sacajawea. Prairie-nigger. Halfbreed. Savages. Tomahawk Chop. 1492. We're still here.

TANIA: What do you think of when I say the word "Lebanon"?

OLGA: Shiites in Jeeps.

ANNA: Long architectural noses. Very sweet desserts. Tom.

ALL: Strife.

TRINKET: Kidnappings.

COCHISE: The cedars of Lebanon.

EVA: Minarets.

TANIA: My bomb pieces and bullet collection. My only doll, Patatina. Blood.

COCHISE: What do you think of when I say the word "Ukraine"?

OLGA: December 1, 1991. Golden domes of Kiev. Golden fields of sunflowers. Golden fields of ripened wheat. More than twenty recipes for *borsht.* Dark bread with salt pork fat and vodka. *Bandura.* Clouds over Chernobyl. No, it's not Russia. Independence. Democracy. It must succeed.

HIROMI: What do you think of when I say the word "Japan"?

(All clap, this time Shinto-like.)

COCHISE: *Hai Karate. Hai Ku.* Monoethnic. Land of the rising sun. Samurai. Sumo. Big money. Paper-thin walls.

19

TANIA: My friends Maiumi and Isumi.

ANNA: The nape of a woman's neck.

TRINKET: Professional pushers for the subway cars.

OLGA: Large tourist groups of short people with a lot of cameras.

EVA: Another planet. Trains like bullets.

HIROMI: Group consensus—

ALL: Hai.

HIROMI: —for a tiny little matter. Economic globalization. Political isolation. Floating weeds.

(All clap and change seats as the Norwegian incantation is repeated. The incantation fades out when they get to their new seats.)

COCHISE: 1973.

ALL: 1973.

COCHISE: February 27. A group of young Native Americans, with the approval of traditional elders, take over the Bureau of Indian Affairs regional office in Wounded Knee, South Dakota—site of the Wounded Knee Massacre. Two weeks later, the FBI and the military are called in. Three Indians are killed and the rest imprisoned.

(All clap.)

TANIA: 1975.

ALL: 1975.

TANIA: A normal day in Beirut. My younger sister Tamira and I are at school. I was in my French reading class. All of a sudden, we hear a huge explosion. All the windows in the classroom shatter. The sisters took us down to the basement, which we had never seen before. They didn't tell us what was going on; they just told us to pray.

ALL *(Reciting the Hail Mary Prayer in French)*:
    Je Vous Salue Marie.
    Je vous salue, Marie, pleine de grâce.
    Le Seigneur est avec vous.
    Vous êtes bénie entre toutes les femmes,
    et Jésus, le fruit de vos entrailles, est béni.
    Sainte Marie, Mère de Dieu,
    priez pour nous, pauvres pécheurs,
    maintenant et à l'heure de notre mort.
    Amen.

TANIA: My mother and my friend Joumana's father came to pick us up at the school. We were waiting for them at the door. Joumana's father was shot and killed right in front of our eyes—the Civil War in Lebanon had begun.

(All clap.)

EVA: 1979.
ALL: 1979.
EVA: The Sandinista Revolution in Nicaragua.

(All clap.)

ANNA: 1989.
ALL: 1989.
ANNA: November 9. The Berlin Wall falls.

(All clap.)

EVA: 1990.
ALL: 1990.
EVA: After eleven years of war, there are free elections in Nicaragua.

(All clap.)

TANIA: 1991.
ALL: 1991.
TANIA: Syria and the U.S. forces are no longer in Lebanon. I still have my bomb pieces and bullet collection.

(All clap.)

TRINKET: 1991.
ALL: 1991. Manila, Philippines.
TRINKET: American military bases become undesirable after the eruption of volcano Pinatubo.

(All clap and rise. Eva rings a bell. Everyone changes places creating a commotion. The bell stops. Everyone sits except for Trinket, who begins to call out in the manner of a street vendor.)

21

TRINKET (*Calling*):
>This way, this way, this way down,
>down to a Filipino bargain town.
>Mix 'em and match 'em and pick 'em and pack 'em!
>All our beloveds will do what you want them to.
>Bachelors, babies, giggling young ladies,
>children, men, women will banish your achies.
>
>This way, this way, this way down!
>Don't buy that Filipino chambermaid doll made in Hong
>>Kong!
>
>We have lots of the real McCoy!
>Flesh an' blood, skin and bones,
>laughing through your dusty homes.
>
>And what's more, we have an
>entire inventory, highest quality!
>English university education, ready to ship to whatever nation.
>BAs, MAs, RNs, PhDs!
>
>If you need love and happiness,
>if you need to battle your illness.
>This way, this way, this way down,
>'cause who will look after your lonely and blue,
>who will look after your children, too.
>
>Bachelors, babies, giggling young ladies,
>children, men, women will banish your achies!
>This way, this way, this way down,
>down to a Filipino bargain town!
>Don't forget—seventy-five percent for meee!

(*Quiet, plaintive flute music begins to play. One by one, each performer recites a poem in his/her native language, while the flute music plays quietly underneath. These poems are not translated, but create a medley of different languages and sounds. The flute music plays throughout.*
>*Olga stands.*)

OLGA: You can choose anything in the world, my son, but you can never choose your heritage.

(Olga sits.
  All clap.)

COCHISE: 1992.
ALL: 1992.
COCHISE: The U.S. still occupies North America.

(All clap.)

ANNA: 1992.
ALL: 1992.
ANNA: October. A performance of *Undesirable Elements* in New York
  City.

*(All clap. An uplifting choral song begins to play softly. It contin-
ues through the finale)*

TANIA: My name is Tania Salmen. I was born in Beirut, Lebanon,
  on the Day of the Dead, the year of Kennedy's assassination.
  Saturday at 8 P.M. A horse named Tania won a race that day.

(She closes her script and stands.)

OLGA: My name is Olga Kyrychenko. I was born in Kiev, Ukraine, on
  November 9, 1937, at 5 P.M. in the afternoon. It was a blazing
  sunset.

(She closes her script and stands.)

TRINKET: My name is Emerald Trinket Monsod. I was born in Quezon City, Philippines, on November 16, 1955, at 9 o'clock in
  the morning. "E," "Emerald," stands for my mother Estrella.
  "T," "Trinket," stands for my father Tomas.

(She closes her script and stands.)

EVA: My name is Eva Gasteazoro. I was born in Chinandega, Nicaragua, on December 12, 1952, at 11:30 P.M., by induced labor.
  The rainy season had ended.

(She closes her script and stands.)

ANNA: My name is Regine Anna Seckinger. I was born in Freiburg, Baden, Germany, at St. Joseph's Hospital on July 7, 1967, at 2:32 P.M. in the midst of a thunderstorm.

(He closes his script and stands.)

HIROMI: My name Hiromi Sakamoto. I was born on September 3, 1961—the thirty-sixth year of Emperor Hirohito—in Sakai City, Osaka Prefecture, Japan. A typhoon night.

(He closes his script and stands.)

COCHISE: My name is Cochise Anderson. Chickasaw. I was born on July 20, 1965, in Los Angeles, California, USA. in the middle of the middle of the summer.

(She closes her script and stands.
Music up. Lights fade down. The performers repeat their gestures from the beginning of the performance, raising, crossing and lowering their arms slowly and gracefully in unison, as the lights fade to blackout. They stand facing the audience in blackout.
Lights up. Each performer takes two bows to each side and then exits the stage.)

END

Children of War

Fairfax, Virginia / 2002

Conceived, written and directed by Ping Chong

IN COLLABORATION WITH:
Farinaz
Yarvin
Abdul
Dereen
Fatu

In 2001, a social service agency in northern Virginia, the Center for Multicultural Human Services, invited me to make a new piece exploring the effects of violence and war on the lives of young people. *Children of War* marks a significant turning point in the history of the *Undesirable Elements* series. It shares its artistic structure and creative history with previous productions of *Undesirable Elements*; however, unlike in previous productions, the common link between the participants is more than shared residency in a local community. The young people in *Children of War* all share another powerful connection: their collective experience of war, which creates the same emotional scars on young people across linguistic, cultural or political divides. While *Undesirable Elements* draws its power from the "simple" act of naming oneself in public, *Children of War* bears witness to the consequences of war on the most vulnerable members of society. Sadly, since 2002, the number of young people living with these experiences has only grown in our country and around the world, and the need to share these stories remains urgent.

—*Ping Chong*

PRODUCTION HISTORY

Children of War premiered at TheaterSpace in the George Mason University Center for the Arts, in Fairfax, Virginia, on December 5, 2002. It was conceived, written and directed by Ping Chong. The performers were Abdul, Dereen, Farinaz, Fatu and Yarvin. The production manager/technical director was John Frautschy and the stage manager was Courtney Golden. The managing director was Bruce Allardice and the project manager was Sara Zatz.

    Children of War was produced by the Center for Multicultural Human Services in Virginia and Ping Chong + Company, in association with the Theater of the First Amendment. *Children of War* was produced with support from the National Endowment for the Arts, MetLife Foundation, and The Ford Foundation.

NOTE: Out of respect for the ages of the participants at the time of the production, only first names are used. Additionally, one original cast member requested that her story not be included for publication, out of concern for her family. The script has therefore been modified from the original in order to accommodate her request. Her narrative has been edited out and lines reassigned.

Six music stands and chairs stand upstage, arranged in a curve around a white semicircle filled with rock salt. Each music stand holds a copy of the script, which the performers read from throughout the performance. None of the performers ever leaves the stage. One chair remains empty throughout the performance.

Lights slowly come up. A haunting Norwegian incantation plays. One at a time, the performers approach their music stands. One by one, they turn to face the audience. As the incantation plays, the performers face the audience and slowly, ritually, raise their arms to the side, then bring them forward, crossing them in front of their bodies, then open them out again, and bring them down to their sides. This motion is repeated slowly and gracefully in unison, as if they are moving through water. The incantation fades out at the end of the gestures.

YARVIN: *¡Vamos a empezar!*
ABDUL: بیایید شروع کنیم!
FARINAZ: بیا شروع کنیم!
FATU: *Le we began!*
DEREEN: با دەست پێ بکەین!
YARVIN (*Translating for all*): Let's get started! Please sit.

(The ensemble sits in their chairs.)

(In Spanish) Mi nombre es Yarvin. Yo nací en el llano Los Patos departamento de la Unión El Salvador.
¿Abdul?

ABDUL *(In Dari):* اسم من عبدل. من به ساعت 3:30 شب 12 اکتوبر سال 1989
به افغانستان در کابل تولد شدم.Farinaz؟
FARINAZ *(In Farsi):* من فریناز هستم و در 23 آوریل 1960 در یک روز آفتابی در
تهران، ایران بهدنیا آمدم. بین سه فرزند خانواده، من بزرگترین
آنها هستم. تولد من در فصل بهار بود. Fatu؟
FATU *(In Krio): Na mi Fatu ha ben bon na salon June 20 and 87 I ben gen get me name from mi granma. An na ben rainseason.*
Dereen?
DEREEN *(In Kurdish):* ناوم دێرینآـه، من کوردم. له ههفدهی مانگی یهکی ساڵی ههزار
و نۆ سهد و ههشتا و حهوت له شاری سلێمانی، له کوردستان له دایک بووم.

(All clap.)

ABDUL: Mohammed.
DEREEN: Lawik.
FATU: Isatu.
YARVIN: Jorge.
FARINAZ: Ali.
ABDUL: Zohal.
DEREEN: Rebeen.
FATU: Foday.
YARVIN: Rita.
FARINAZ: Abdolah.
ABDUL: Ahmed.
DEREEN: Sana.
FATU: Adama.
YARVIN: Santos.
FARINAZ: Amir.
ABDUL: Karim.
DEREEN: Rezhen.
FATU: Sorie.
YARVIN: Maria.
FARINAZ: Fatemeh.
ABDUL: Bibigol.
DEREEN: Raz.
FATU: Abibaatu.
YARVIN: Pedro.
FARINAZ: Zohreh.

(All clap ten times.)

FATU: Sierra Leone.
ALL: Sierra Leone.
FATU: 1492.
ALL: 1492.
FATU: Pedro de Sintra.
ALL: Pedro de Sintra.
FARINAZ: Pedro de Sintra, a Portuguese explorer, maps a mountainous peninsula and calls it:
YARVIN: Serra Lyoa,
FARINAZ: or Lion Mountain.
FATU: I am from Sierra Leone.

(All clap.)

YARVIN: These are the people who made my life miserable:
ABDUL: Abuela Tina,
FATU: Maria,
FARINAZ: Christina,
DEREEN: Pedro,
FATU: Manuel.
YARVIN: These are the people who sustained me with their kindness:
ABDUL: Martin,
FARINAZ: Francisco,
FATU: Santos,
DEREEN: Emma,
FARINAZ: Lidia,
FATU: José,
ABDUL: Ellen.

(All clap.)

The Kurds.
DEREEN *(In Kurdish)*: خەڵکێکی بێ وڵات!
FARINAZ *(Translating)*: A people without a homeland.
ABDUL: Kurdistan.
DEREEN *(In Kurdish)*: ناوچەیەک کە بەشێک لە ئێراق، ئێران، سووریا، ئەرمینیا، تورکیا و ئازەربایجان دەگرێتەوە.
FARINAZ *(Translating)*: A region that includes parts of Iraq, Iran, Syria, Armenia, Turkey and Azerbaijan.

DEREEN *(In Kurdish)*: .من کوردم و ولاتم نییه

FARINAZ *(Translating)*: He is a Kurd without a homeland.

> *(All clap ten times. Blackout.*
> *Beat.*
> *Lights up.)*

DEREEN: 1867.

ALL: 1867.

DEREEN: By 1867, the Kurds, an ancient people in the Middle East, are reduced to a handful of kingdoms, which are systematically destroyed by the Ottoman Turks and the Persians.

FATU: 1895.

ABDUL: 1895.

FATU: The British colonize Sierra Leone; they will rule for the next sixty-six years.

DEREEN: 1921.

FARINAZ: 1921.

DEREEN: With the fall of the Ottoman or Turkish Empire and the end of World War II, my people's plea for independence results in a treaty, but it is not ratified. Instead, France and Britain divide Kurdistan for themselves.

FATU: It is the beginning of the politics of oil.

FATU: 1961.

DEREEN: 1961.

FARINAZ: Sierra Leone.

FATU: After sixty-six years, Sierra Leone gains its independence.

FARINAZ: English becomes the official language.

FATU AND YARVIN: 1964.

FARINAZ: 1964.

DEREEN: Sierra Leone.

FATU: After four years of peaceful rule, there is a coup d'état:

YARVIN: a military takeover.

FATU: From now on, there will be,

FARINAZ: one corrupt government after another,

YARVIN: one bad leader after another,

ALL: over and over again.

FARINAZ: 1966.

ABDUL: 1966.

YARVIN: Tehran, Iran.

FARINAZ: Although Rahmat Sheybani comes from a wealthy family, he takes advantage of no one. Even though he has servants, they eat at his dinner table, with his family, as equals. When the servants' children are old enough, he sends them to the same school as his own children. Rahmat's goodness is evident in every breath of his life. He is my grandfather.

FARINAZ AND YARVIN: 1968.

FATU: 1968.

DEREEN: Tehran, Iran.

FARINAZ: After finishing his master's degree in the United States, my father returns to Iran to work in the oil industry. The shah's brother, Prince Mahmoud Reza Pahlavi, who he met in the United States, says to him:

DEREEN: "Dariush, if you want to rise in Iran I will help you throw a party at your house. I will make all the party arrangements and I will invite all the important guests. You have to know the right people if you want to get ahead."

FARINAZ: But my father knows he lives in a corrupt society with corrupt leaders. He refuses to throw the party. He doesn't want the help of corrupt men.

DEREEN: 1976.

YARVIN: 1976.

ABDUL: 1976.

FATU: Sulaimaniya, Kurdistan.

DEREEN: Khala Shahab, a Kurdish man, is captured and assassinated by the Iraqi government. He is a member of the Patriotic Union of Kurdistan, which promotes the independence of the Kurdish people from Iraq. His nephew, Dillshad, will join the independence movement, too. Although I am not yet born, Dillshad and I will share a history.

FARINAZ: 1977.

ABDUL: 1977.

FARINAZ: I return to Iran after a year in the United States as a foreign exchange student. The situation in my country grows worse. The rich grow richer and the poor grow poorer. My father openly discusses the injustices and oppression in our country with us, but he warns:

YARVIN: "Do not talk about this outside our home. It is dangerous to do so."

FARINAZ: People who openly criticize the shah's government are tortured or murdered or both. Many just disappear.

DEREEN: 1977.

YARVIN: 1977.

FATU: Sulaimaniya, Kurdistan.

DEREEN: A young college girl named Shayan is walking down a city street. In the opposite direction, Dillshad is also walking down the street. Their eyes meet from afar. Their eyes have met before, but dating is forbidden. What can they do?

FARINAZ: 1978.

ABDUL: 1978.

YARVIN: October 1978.

ALL (*Chanting*): Death to the shah! Death to the shah! Death to the shah!

FARINAZ: The people of Iran are fed up, but the shah is beyond listening. He slaughters his own people in the street. There is blood everywhere.

FARINAZ AND YARVIN: 1979.

FATU: 1979.

FARINAZ: The Shah of Iran goes into exile. People are dancing in the streets, cars are honking their horns, and people are celebrating everywhere. I am filled with happiness. But the new regime of the Ayatollah Ruhollah Khomeini is a new nightmare within an old nightmare.

DEREEN: 1979.

FATU: 1979.

YARVIN: August 1979.

DEREEN: Two years pass. Dillshad and Shayan still pass each other on the streets of Sulaimaniya. Their eyes still meet, but that is all. One day, the phone rings in Shayan's home. It is Dillshad. He says:

ABDUL: "May I marry you?"

DEREEN: They will be my parents.

FARINAZ: 1980.

YARVIN: 1980.

FARINAZ: From 1978 through 1980, I am a member of an underground political movement—first against the shah, then against the Khomeini regime. I am committed to working for the good of the ordinary people, but it is dangerous. My friend Abu is killed. He was a freedom fighter for the Kurdish people in Iran.

DEREEN: 1980.

FARINAZ: 1980.

YARVIN: September 22, 1980.

DEREEN: Iraq goes to war with Iran.

ABDUL: There are no good guys in this war.

YARVIN: The first world doesn't care if a few hundred thousand third-world people die.

FARINAZ: They profit from the war by selling weapons to both sides.

DEREEN: This includes:

FATU: France,

YARVIN: Israel,

FARINAZ: the Soviet Union,

ABDUL: and the United States.

FARINAZ: 1981.

DEREEN: 1981.

FARINAZ: I take an interest in nursing, in healing people. I am working as a nurse's aide at a hospital. At the same time, I am still working for the underground movement. One night before going to work, I try to deliver flyers that criticize the government. I wrap them up like a birthday present so that I won't get caught. As I get into a taxi, a woman stops me:

FATU: "I want to search your bag."

FARINAZ: The taxi driver, who knows me, says:

YARVIN: "Sister, I know her. She works at the hospital."

FARINAZ: The woman finds my gift-wrapped flyers:

FATU: "What's this?"

FARINAZ: "It's a birthday present."

YARVIN: One,

DEREEN: two,

YARVIN: three seconds pass.

FARINAZ: The woman lets me go, but just as I leave, a man who is with her says:

DEREEN: "Open the gift."

ALL: 1981.

ABDUL: 1981.

FARINAZ: For four days and nights, I am interrogated and tortured:

YARVIN: "If you tell us the names of the people in the movement, we'll let you go."

FATU: "If you reject what you believe in and publicly join Khomeini's side, we'll let you go."

FARINAZ: My grandfather's spirit stands beside me:

DEREEN: "Farinaz, you have to have a heart. Focus with your heart and you will know what is right and what is wrong."

FARINAZ: I refuse to join the other side:

YARVIN: "Farinaz, you are sentenced to ten years in prison."

FARINAZ: My mother doesn't know if I'm dead or alive.

(All clap.)

FATU: 1985.

ABDUL: 1985.

YARVIN: Sierra Leone.

FARINAZ: Mounting debt,

YARVIN: deteriorating infrastructure,

FARINAZ: unpaid workers,

YARVIN: mounting discontent,

FARINAZ: deteriorating services,

YARVIN: increasing factionalism.

FATU: Attempts at financial, administrative and political reform in Sierra Leone fail.

FARINAZ: 1986.

DEREEN: 1986.

FARINAZ: My fellow prisoners plan an uprising. I warn:

YARVIN: "Have you forgotten? Don't underestimate the power of the regime. They will slaughter us."

FARINAZ: The uprising comes to pass. Five of us oppose it, but we have to go along. It fails. Each of us is blindfolded and put into a space we call a "grave," just wide enough to sit up in. We are forbidden to move for the entire day. If we move, we are beaten. The leaders of the uprising are the first to cave in. The five who opposed the uprising stand fast. For nine months, we remain blindfolded in the "graves." The biggest lesson I learned from this experience is that every human being has a choice. Every human being is in charge of shaping their own reality.

ABDUL: 1987.

FARINAZ: 1987.

DEREEN: War in Afghanistan.

ABDUL: A young man is wounded. In the hospital, he meets a young nurse. The young man asks:

DEREEN: "What is your name?"

YARVIN: "Rahela."

ABDUL: If they had not met that day, I would not be here now.

(All clap.)

DEREEN: 1987.

FATU: 1987.

FARINAZ: January 17, 1987.

FATU: Bombs explode.

YARVIN: Windows shatter in Dereen's house.

ABDUL: The phone line dies.

FARINAZ: Dereen's aunt is wounded.

DEREEN: On this day, I am born.

(All clap.)

YARVIN: 1987.

ABDUL: 1987.

DEREEN: El Salvador.

YARVIN: The sky is painted purple.

FATU: There are white clouds in the sky. On the ground, there is a painted blue lake with painted frogs and painted ducks.

FARINAZ: In front of this backdrop sits a real family: a mother, father and some children. Everybody faces front.

YARVIN: Nobody smiles.

FATU: Then there is a flash. Nobody smiles because being photographed is serious.

YARVIN: My mother is a photographer. I am three years old.

YARVIN AND FATU: 1988.

ABDUL: 1988.

YARVIN: More than seven members of my mother's family are killed in the civil war in El Salvador. My mother wants to go to the United States. She says:

FARINAZ: "If you work hard there, you can have anything you want."

DEREEN: 1988.

FARINAZ: 1988.

YARVIN: 1988.

FATU: August 8, 1988.

DEREEN: The Iran-Iraq War ends.

FARINAZ: The Kurdish people's fight for independence continues.

DEREEN: Now, the Iraqi government can turn its attention to killing my people.

FARINAZ: Women, children and men are killed.

YARVIN: Entire villages are bombed.

FARINAZ: 1989.

YARVIN: 1989.

ABDUL: Tehran, Iran.

FARINAZ: The Khomeini regime decides to slaughter all the political prisoners,

FATU: male and female,

DEREEN: in all the major prisons.

ALL: Mass executions.

FARINAZ: The women's prison is next, but halfway through the slaughter, international pressure stops the bloodshed. I am freed. When

I entered prison, my mother had only a few gray hairs. When I leave prison, her hair is almost all gray.

ABDUL: 1989.

DEREEN: 1989.

ABDUL: Afghanistan.

FARINAZ: After ten years of war, the Russians withdraw from Afghanistan but,

YARVIN: war continues in the countryside—

ABDUL: tribe against tribe.

YARVIN: 1990.

FATU: 1990.

DEREEN: El Salvador.

YARVIN: One day, I am playing outside with my brother and sister. My mother says:

FATU: "Come with me."

YARVIN: We walk with her and her boyfriend, Martin, to the blue-green-and-white bus stop. She says (*In Spanish*), "*Me voy a Los Estados Unidos. Es posible ganar mucho dinero allá. El dinero es verde. Voy a regresar, pero no se cuando.*"

FATU (*Translating*): "I'm going to the United States. You can make lots of money there. Money is green there. I'll be back, but I don't know when."

YARVIN: We are very excited. She hugs each of us. Then, we watch the bus go away, get smaller and smaller.

YARVIN AND FATU: 1990.

ABDUL: 1990.

YARVIN: My grandmother and aunt move into my mother's house with Martin. In the beginning, everything is good. Then my grandmother and aunt start to beat us. I try to protect my younger brother and sister; they beat me even more. This goes on for four or five times a week, every week. Martin tries to stop them. He is kind to us, but they wait until he goes to work to attack. I am six years old.

(*All clap.*)

DEREEN: 1991.

FATU: 1991.

DEREEN: George Bush, Sr. promises assistance to the Kurds if they stage a major uprising against Saddam Hussein. They do, but the assistance never comes. The Kurds are left to face superior forces alone.

FATU: 1991.

FARINAZ: 1991.

DEREEN: Freetown, Sierra Leone.

FATU: Life is hard in Sierra Leone. My father goes to America. I think to myself:

YARVIN: How can he go to America? He's not rich.

DEREEN: 1991.

FARINAZ: 1991.

DEREEN: My father is playing soccer with me in our yard. He is carrying me on his shoulder. We are laughing a lot. My father is tucking me into bed and telling me a bedtime story. My father has green eyes and a big mustache. I love my father. I am four years old.

DEREEN AND ABDUL: 1991.

FARINAZ: 1991.

FATU: 1991.

FARINAZ: 1991.

DEREEN: The Iraqi army attacks Sulaimaniya again.

YARVIN: Three million people flee the city.

DEREEN: My family drives to the Iraq-Iran border but most families go by foot. There are so many people fleeing that our car moves really slowly. It begins to rain, the temperature drops. The mountainside is a forest of burnt trees and brown mud. Just as we reach the mountains, helicopters begin bombing the city. If we had not left Sulaimaniya that day, I would not be here now.

(All clap.)

1991.

ABDUL: 1991.

DEREEN: The bitter cold and the icy rain continue. A woman with a sick child, soaking in the rain, begs my mother:

FATU: "Food, please, give me food. Please give me a blanket. Help me."

DEREEN: My mother gives her some biscuits, but we do not have an extra blanket to share. Then both my brother and I get sick, too. My father says:

FARINAZ: "Either we die in this barren place, or we take our chances and go back."

DEREEN: We go back after five days and nights.

1991.

FARINAZ: 1991.

FATU: 1991.

DEREEN: Even though international forces stop the killing, we are afraid. As we drive back slowly into the city, we see bodies everywhere.

YARVIN: The streets are stained with blood.

FARINAZ: Many houses have been burnt to the ground.

YARVIN: It is a ghost town.

DEREEN: Through the windows of the car, we watch soldiers looting the homes of our friends. We have no idea which ones are dead or alive.

(All clap.)

YARVIN: 1992.

FATU: 1992.

ABDUL: El Salvador.

YARVIN: The beatings continue. I try to run away with my brother and sister, but where can three small children go? When we come back, they don't beat us for a while. Then the nightmare begins all over again. It's as if they can't help themselves. I dream that one day I will find a place where nobody will beat us again and people will be kind to us. I think to myself:

FATU: I must be a very bad child for this to happen to me. I must be very bad.

FARINAZ: 1992.

ABDUL: 1992.

FARINAZ: April 29, 1992.

YARVIN: Sierra Leone.

FATU: Young soldiers take power from the latest "bad" government, but they are just as bad.

FARINAZ: Sierra Leone collapses into civil war.

FATU: 1992.

ABDUL: 1992.

FARINAZ: I don't want to go to the United States, but my boyfriend comes back to get me and, after seven and a half years in prison, I am too numb to resist. After a while, I go to Marymount University in Arlington, Virginia, to resume my studies in nursing.

DEREEN: 1992.

FATU: 1992.

FARINAZ: November 28, 1992.

DEREEN: There has been no electricity for five days. My mother cooks dinner while there is still light. She makes hamburgers for us and only rice and potatoes for herself and my father. When dinner is ready, she wakes my father, who is napping. He says:

FARINAZ: "Why didn't you wake me earlier? I shouldn't sleep so much."

DEREEN: We sit down in the only heated room in the house and eat by candlelight. My father says:

FARINAZ: "I'm starving to death!"

DEREEN: Just as my father is about to take the first bite, there is a knock at the door. My mother says:

YARVIN: "Who can it be at this time of night?"

FARINAZ: "Why are you worried? Calm down, calm down."

DEREEN: My father goes to the bedroom and gets a pistol.

FATU: One,

ABDUL: two,

YARVIN: three eternities pass.

DEREEN: My father opens the door. My mother follows behind with a candle. I am clutching my mother's dress. Out of the darkness a voice comes:

FATU (*In Kurdish*): تۆ دڵشادیت؟

ABDUL (*Translating*): "Toa Dillshady?"

FARINAZ: "Yes, I am."

DEREEN: I hear gunshots. They light up my father's face. Bullets are whizzing in all directions.

My father falls. My mother screams. In the darkness, my mother asks:

YARVIN: "Dillshad! Dillshad! Did they shoot you? Have you been wounded?"

FARINAZ: "Yes."

DEREEN: I escape from my mother's arms and run to him. He is bleeding badly. My father struggles to get up. He wants to tell us he loves us. Then he falls again. My father dies. I don't have a chance to tell him I love him. I am five years old.

1992.

FATU: 1992.

DEREEN: My mother falls into a deep depression. Only when I am diagnosed with typhoid is she able to come back to life. She must take me to Baghdad, the Iraqi capital, to save me.

At every Iraqi checkpoint, she must suffer insults because she is a Kurd.

(*All clap ten times.*)

43

FARINAZ (*In Farsi*): لطفا بایستید

(All rise. They change seats, walking single file around the outer perimeter of the semi-circle as the Norwegian incantation is repeated.)

لطفا بنشینید

(All sit and open their scripts.)

ABDUL: 1992.

ALL: 1992.

DEREEN: War comes to Afghanistan again.

ABDUL: A TV station is bombed. We watch it burn from our yard. My mother covers the windows with pillows.

FARINAZ: It is no longer safe in Abdul's house.

ABDUL: We move.

ABDUL AND DEREEN: 1993.

FATU: 1993.

ABDUL: One month later,

YARVIN: the war starts again.

ABDUL: At 11 P.M. my father is listening to the news on the radio.

FARINAZ: All of the sudden, there is a huge explosion.

YARVIN: The building next door is hit by a missile.

ABDUL: Glass shatters all over my father, but he is not hurt. Guns are firing everywhere. We run from one room to another—

FARINAZ: more missiles whistle by,

YARVIN: more explosions,

FATU: more gunfire.

ABDUL: We run down to the basement, where everyone else has already gone. We are very afraid.

(All clap.)

1993.

YARVIN: 1993.

ABDUL: My father decides we must leave Afghanistan. With a bicycle pump, he blows air into the tires of his car.

FARINAZ: Three families, including Abdul's, leave together for Pakistan.

YARVIN: Twelve people pile into a small car.

ABDUL: We have to pass many checkpoints. We don't know who is enemy or friend.

FARINAZ: Abdul's father bribes his way past.

ABDUL: We leave our (*In Dari*) وطن

FATU (*In Krio*): *Me country wa bon.*

YARVIN (*In Spanish*): *Tierra natal.*

DEREEN (*In Kurdish*): ولّات.

FARINAZ (*In Farsi*): وطن

ALL (*Translating*): Homeland.

(*All clap.*)

YARVIN: 1994.

FATU: 1994.

DEREEN: El Salvador.

YARVIN: My mother wants me to come to America. I go to the same blue-green-and-white bus stop. My brother, sister and Martin come to say good-bye. My grandmother and aunt don't come. I take the bus to San Salvador—the capitol of El Salvador—

FATU: then a bus to Guatemala,

FARINAZ: then a bus to Mexico, and then to Los Angeles by air.

YARVIN: I am very tired when I arrive. I am nine years old.

YARVIN AND ABDUL: 1994.

FATU: 1994.

DEREEN: LAX, Los Angeles.

YARVIN: After three years, I finally see my mother again, but I don't recognize her:

FATU: "You're not my mom! You're so fat!"

YARVIN: She laughs. Then she introduces Francisco, her husband. I ask:

FATU: "What about Martin in El Salvador?"

FARINAZ: "Don't worry about him. He'll be okay. Just keep quiet."

ABDUL: 1994.

YARVIN: 1994.

ABDUL: I ask my father:

DEREEN: "Can I go back to our apartment in Kabul?"

FARINAZ: "Why?"

DEREEN: "I want to pick up a toy that I left behind, a remote-controlled tank."

ABDUL: My father says:

FARINAZ: "The building is gone. It is dust now."

(*All clap.*)

FATU: 1994.

YARVIN: 1994.

FARINAZ: Sierra Leone.

FATU: One faction of the civil war comes to Freetown, my city, to catch soldiers. They take boys as young as twelve years old and turn them into killers. This is how they do it:

FARINAZ: cut small slits in their skin,

YARVIN: rub cocaine in the cuts.

FARINAZ: It makes the boys better killers.

YARVIN: Kill their families in front of them.

ABDUL: It makes the boys better killers.

FARINAZ: There are now thousands of children raping, stealing and killing in Sierra Leone.

YARVIN: 1994.

FATU: 1994.

YARVIN: One day, I ask my mother:

FATU: "Why was my grandmother so mean?"

YARVIN: She says:

FARINAZ: "Her mother left her when she was young, and she was sexually abused by her dad."

YARVIN: A few months later, my mother turns into my grandmother, and the beatings begin all over again. She screams:

FATU: "You're not my daughter! You're just a dog I picked out of the trash."

FARINAZ: Yarvin's nightmare begins all over again.

ABDUL: 1994.

FARINAZ: 1994.

ABDUL: Life is hard in Pakistan. There is no money. My parents have no work. They have to sell their belongings:

FATU: a typewriter,

DEREEN: an Afghani rug,

YARVIN: antiques,

FARINAZ: four hundred prayer beads made of precious stones,

DEREEN: a gift from people returning from Hajj.

ABDUL: My father is very unhappy. He lost his job, his house and his country.

FATU: 1994.

YARVIN: 1994.

FATU: My father sends things home to us from America:

ABDUL: shoes,

YARVIN: clothes,

ALL: Avon lotion!

FATU: My friends ask:

YARVIN: "What did you get from America this time?"

(All clap.)

ABDUL: 1995.

FATU: 1995.

YARVIN: Pakistan.

ABDUL: My father is selling snow cones on the street. Five Pakistani men start a fight with him. One says:

FATU: "Why don't you go back to your country?"

ABDUL: Then they beat up my father. In Pakistan, I have only Afghani friends.

YARVIN: 1995.

ABDUL: 1995.

YARVIN: I run away to a neighbor, Lidia, who is kind to me. She wants to adopt me, but she says:

FARINAZ: "Yarvin, you have to call your mom so she doesn't worry about you."

YARVIN: I go home. She doesn't beat me for a month. Then it starts all over again.

DEREEN: 1996.

FARINAZ: 1996.

DEREEN: The UN declares Sulaimaniya a no-fly zone. We think the Kurdish people are safe under UN protection, but we are wrong.

ABDUL: Iraqi soldiers attack again,

FATU: death comes again.

DEREEN: Because my mother works for the United Nations at this time, we flee to the UN compound. News comes from UN command that we will be evacuated from Iraq:

YARVIN: "Prepare yourself to leave."

FARINAZ: "Sell your possessions so you will have cash."

DEREEN AND FATU: 1996.

YARVIN: 1996.

FATU: Two days later.

DEREEN: I am leaving my country. I want to bring everything with me, but I can't. Instead, I take:

YARVIN: a stuffed black-and-white bunny,

ABDUL: a beanie baby giraffe,

FATU: and a black-and-brown stuffed dog.

DEREEN: My mother takes my father's photograph and a small photo album. We get into a bus crowded with exhausted people and ride for hours. When we get to the Turkey-Iraq border, we cross a small wooden bridge. That small wooden bridge is the space between home and exile. Everyone looks back and cries. I am nine years old.

1996.

FATU: 1996.

DEREEN: It is night. It is dark. Where are we? It is pouring rain. There are hundreds and hundreds of tents in a row, glowing like lanterns. In the confusion and exhaustion we are told to find a place to rest.

YARVIN: What place?

FATU: Where?

DEREEN: Wet with rain, we walk through the mud, not knowing where to go, carrying all our possessions. Then:

FARINAZ: "Shayan, is that you?"

YARVIN: "Yes, it is."

FARINAZ: "Come and stay in our tent."

DEREEN: We have found friends. Now we can rest.

(*All clap ten times. Blackout.*
Beat.
Lights up on Fatu as she sings a song in Krio about the suffering of the Sierra Leonean people in the civil war.
Beat.)

Yarvin?

YARVIN: Yes, Dereen?

DEREEN: What do you think of when you hear the words "El Salvador"?

YARVIN: I think of *carne asada*, which is grilled meat. *Papusas*, which are like *empanadas* made of corn flour with meat and cheese. The games I used to play with my brother and sister. The warm weather. Fireworks at Christmas. After all these years, I think of El Salvador as a dream that I cannot go back to.

ABDUL: Fatu?

FATU: Yes, Abdul?

ABDUL: What do you think of when I say the words "Sierra Leone"?

FATU: I think of peanut butter cake, cassava leaf sauce, and *fufu*, which is cassava porridge that I *still* eat with my hands. I think of my school uniform, which I miss. I think of respect for elders, respect for teachers. I think of my grandmother's songs. My friend, Fanta, who was killed in the war. I think of the silence of the dead.

YARVIN: Fatu?

FATU: Yes, Yarvin?

YARVIN: What do you think of when I say the word "war"?

FATU: I think whoever is fighting should put us on a plane and let us go, and when they finish fighting, bring us back.

YARVIN: Farinaz?

FARINAZ: Yes, Yarvin?

YARVIN: What do you think of when I say the word "Iran"?

FARINAZ: I think of climbing cherry trees in the summer, and the Caspian Sea. I think of the embrace, the comfort, the support of family. I think of New Year's traditions, like setting the Haft Seen table, visiting elders and receiving gifts of money from them. I think of the kindness of Iranian people. I think of being robbed of this kindness because of fear and oppression. I think of the death of trust. I think of my comrades who died because of their beliefs: Yusef, Mansur, Abu and many more.

FATU: Abdul?

ABDUL: Yes, Fatu?

FATU: What do you think of when I say the word "Afghanistan"?

ABDUL: My grandparents. The smell of roses. The roses here don't smell as strong. I miss the freedom of playing outside our house. *Kabuli Pilau*, a rice dish with meat, carrots and raisins. I think of riding horses under a big, open sky.

FARINAZ: Abdul?

ABDUL: Yes, Farinaz?

FARINAZ: What do you think of when you hear the word "war"?

ABDUL: I think of wives without husbands, children without parents. People forced out of their homes. I think two leaders of a war should fight by themselves, instead of so many people dying for nothing. I think of never fighting, even with children in school.

FARINAZ: Dereen?

DEREEN: Yes, Farinaz?

FARINAZ: What do you think of when I say the word "Kurdistan"?

DEREEN: I think of the memories that pull me back to Alab, a valley in Kurdistan, full of sorrow and tears. People who live as strangers in their own land. The history of a population without a country. I think of mountains under a smoky sky. I think of my dad, and the dreams that went with him to his grave. I think of the silence of the dead.

(Ten bells are heard.)

(*In Kurdish*) تکایه هەڵسن

(*All rise. They change seats, walking single file around the outer perimeter of the semi-circle as the Norwegian incantation is repeated.*)

(*In Kurdish*) تکایه دانیشن

(*All sit and open their scripts.*)

YARVIN: 1996.

ALL: 1996.

FARINAZ: Rockville, Maryland.

YARVIN: I am standing at a bus stop with an old African-American woman and a Latina woman. I overhear the African-American woman say:

FARINAZ: "You foreigners don't have the right to be here if you're not going to learn English. Why don't you go back to your own country?"

DEREEN: 1996.

FATU: 1996.

ALL: Welcome to America!

DEREEN: Everybody on the American TV shows we watched in Sulaimaniya was blond-haired and blue-eyed, but when we arrive in America, they are not.

ALL: Welcome to the *real* America!

(*All clap.*)

DEREEN AND FATU: 1996.

YARVIN: 1996.

FARINAZ: Annandale Elementary School.

DEREEN: I don't speak English. It's hard. Some kids think I'm weird because I'm quiet in class, I look different, I have black eyes and black hair, and I am polite.

FATU: "Where are you from?"

DEREEN: "I'm from Kurdistan."

FATU: "Where's that?"

DEREEN: When I point to Iraq on a map he says:

FATU: "You must be for Saddam Hussein."

DEREEN: My mother says:

FARINAZ: "Some people are surprised when I tell them I have a degree in engineering. They assume I am uneducated. They assume

I come from a backwards place, which Sulaimaniya is not. They wonder out loud if I learned to wear Western clothes here, which I did not. I wonder who is actually ignorant."

(*All clap.*)

FATU: 1998.
ALL: 1998.
FATU: Who are the rebels?
DEREEN: They are monsters.
ABDUL: They are boys who kill.
YARVIN: They are boys who burn people to death in their houses.
FARINAZ: They are boys who chop innocent people's hands off for fun.
ALL: They're monsters.
FATU: War comes closer to home, to Freetown.
YARVIN: 1998.
FATU: 1998.
DEREEN: Ocean City, Maryland.
YARVIN: I go to Ocean City with my mom and two men I don't know well. We have a nice day at the beach. When evening comes, we go back to our motel room. My mother says:
FATU: "I am going outside for a walk with Marvin."
YARVIN: I tell her I want to go, too, but she tells me to stay with the other man, Manuel. Thirty minutes later he grabs me and pins me down.
FARINAZ: "Don't scream. This is what your mother promised me. I paid for you."
YARVIN: I am fourteen years old.

(*All clap.*)

YARVIN AND FARINAZ: 1998.
ALL: 1998.
YARVIN: My mother kicks me out of the house. I have no money or clothes. I walk a long way to my cousin Santos's house. Santos says:
FARINAZ: "Your mom was raped when she was about your age. She had you when she was fourteen years old. Then her mother kicked her out."
    1998.
FATU: 1998.
YARVIN: Arlington, Virginia.

FARINAZ: Almost ten years have passed since I was in prison. The distance between the present and that traumatic past allows me to reflect on that experience. When I think back, I am totally amazed by the complexity of human behavior. We prisoners were all in the same situation, yet each human being reacted so differently. For me, that is amazing and I need to understand why. Where will this need lead me?

(All clap.)

YARVIN: 1998.

ALL: 1998.

YARVIN: Santos is kind to me. After I get a job he teaches me how to—

ABDUL: save money,

DEREEN: pay bills,

FARINAZ: and buy groceries—

YARVIN: how to take care of myself. I am ready to get my own apartment. I don't want to take advantage of Santos's kindness. Before I go, I tell him:

FATU: "From now on, my name is Melissa Coreas and I am twenty-one years old."

YARVIN: I get a job at Burger King, first as a cashier, then as a manager. I am the youngest manager they've ever had, but they don't know it. At work I present myself as a happy, outgoing person. They don't know how much sadness I carry inside me.

FATU: 1998.

DEREEN: 1998.

FATU: Abu is fourteen years old. He has a pointed nose and big, friendly eyes. Abu and I make a deal. If I don't want to do my homework, he does it for me, and I give him fruit.

YARVIN: Fruit for homework,

DEREEN: homework for fruit—

FATU: it's a *really* good deal.

(All clap.)

FATU AND ABDUL: 1999.

ALL: 1999.

FATU: I am in my neighbor's yard.

FARINAZ: They had just dug a well.

FATU: I am standing next to Abu, watching.

YARVIN: All of the sudden, there is a popping sound.

FATU: Everybody scatters.

FARINAZ: Abu falls.

FATU: I drag him into my neighbor's bedroom and hide with him under the bed. When the shooting stops, I pull Abu out. I am covered in blood.

FARINAZ: Abu is dead.

FATU: I am eleven years old.
    1999.

YARVIN: 1999.

FATU: When a Muslim person dies in Sierra Leone,

DEREEN: he or she is buried the same day, a few hours later.

FARINAZ: It takes three hours for Abu's funeral procession to get to the cemetery because of sniper fire. His body is put in the ground and then the coffin will be used again for the next to die.

FATU: So many people are dying.

(All clap.)

YARVIN: 1999.

ALL: 1999.

FATU: Arlington, Virginia.

YARVIN: I move in with a young man named José. He is kind to me, but he doesn't know who I am. He thinks I am Melissa Coreas and that I am twenty-one years old, that I am a happy, outgoing person.

YARVIN AND FATU: 1999.

FARINAZ: 1999.

YARVIN: I am pregnant. One day after José comes home from work, I decide to tell him my whole story.

ABDUL: Five,

DEREEN: ten,

FARINAZ: fifteen minutes pass.

YARVIN: He is upset and I am upset. Will I lose this kind man in my life, too? But then José says:

DEREEN: "I am not going to let anything bad happen to you. I am going to protect you."

(All clap.)

FATU: 1999.

ALL: 1999.

ABDUL: 1999.

YARVIN: 1999.

FATU: Sierra Leone.

FARINAZ: Hell descends on Freetown.

FATU: No one knows who is shooting whom.

YARVIN: It is complete chaos.

FATU: But when the fighting stops, life goes on. When I go to the market place, I cover my face with ash and wear old clothes to look like a crazy person. This way, the boy soldiers will leave me alone.

DEREEN: Life goes on.

ABDUL: You still have to eat.

FARINAZ: You still have to sleep.

YARVIN: You still have to work.

FARINAZ: You still have to laugh.

FATU: But I am too scared to sleep. I am too scared to eat.

FATU AND DEREEN: 1999.

ABDUL: 1999.

FATU: We hear screaming in the market. Everybody runs.

FARINAZ: "Do you want a short sleeve or a long sleeve?"

FATU: That is what the boy killers ask.

FARINAZ: If you say "long sleeve," they chop off your entire arm.

YARVIN: If you say "short sleeve," they chop off your arm at the elbow.

FATU: People run past me, screaming, with no arms.

(All clap.)

ABDUL: 1999.

ALL: 1999.

ABDUL: We win a lottery to go to the United States, but when my mother learns we need ten thousand U.S. dollars to go, she almost tears the letter apart.

FARINAZ: 1999.

YARVIN: 1999.

FATU: Time passes.

FARINAZ: I am a nursing intern at Walter Reed Hospital. As an intern, you are too busy—checking the charts and delivering the medicines of more patients than you can handle. You have very little time to actually sit and listen to the fears and worries of patients, which somebody should be doing. Over time, I observe and learn that telling your story is an important part of the healing process. I notice that a patient's state of mind directly affects their physical recovery. Where will this interest lead me?

(All clap.)

FATU: 1999.

ALL: 1999.

FATU: My uncle says:

FARINAZ: "You have to leave. It is not safe here anymore."

FATU: We leave my neighborhood. My family takes what they can carry—the carpet we sleep on, the cooking pot. The streets outside are full of rotting bodies. Dogs are eating them. I see my friend's mother dead. My shoe gets stuck in a body; the smell is horrible. We reach a bombed-out house and sleep together on our carpet. We have no food or water. We are very tired.

FATU AND YARVIN: 1999.

DEREEN: 1999.

FATU: I can't sleep. I can't eat. I am afraid. My girlfriends, Kadiatu and Sally, have been raped. Sally's mother is killed in front of her. My girlfriend Fanta is taken to be a rebel bride. I think to myself:

YARVIN: Maybe if I join the rebels, I will be safe.

(All clap.)

FATU: 1999.

ALL: 1999.

FATU: Finally my aunt gets enough money for us to leave. All five of my sisters, my brother and I go to Guinea, like so many other refugees. Then we go to Senegal for visas to the United States.

YARVIN: 2000.

ABDUL: 2000.

YARVIN: I go to Arlington Social Services and tell them my whole story. Afterwards, they won't let me leave because I am a minor and six months pregnant. I'm scared. What will they do to me?

(All clap.)

YARVIN AND ABDUL: 2000.

ALL: 2000.

FARINAZ: "Yarvin, don't be afraid. We are going to put you in a foster home. You will be safe there, okay?"

YARVIN: I don't want to lose José. I don't want to lose my baby. I don't want to lose my freedom. I think to myself:

FATU: What if my foster mother hates Hispanics?

FARINAZ: What if she doesn't like me?

ABDUL: What if she beats me?

FATU: 2000.

FARINAZ: 2000.

FATU: We arrive at JFK airport. I don't recognize my father. He is so fat! It has been nine years since I saw him.

ABDUL: There is no death in America!

YARVIN: America is like Heaven!

FATU: When I see the tall buildings and city lights, I think to myself:

YARVIN: They were right. America really is the first world!

(All clap.)

FATU AND DEREEN: 2000.

ALL: 2000.

FATU: When we finally arrive at my father's house, I am amazed. In our house in Sierra Leone, there was no glass in our windows,

ABDUL: no running water,

YARVIN: no refrigerator,

DEREEN: no telephone.

FATU: In Sierra Leone, the children slept together on a carpet on the floor. Here, I sleep in a real bed for the first time. It is the first time I feel safe in a long time. I fall into a deep, deep sleep.

YARVIN: 2000.

DEREEN: 2000.

FARINAZ: Fairfax, Virginia.

YARVIN: We drive to the foster home. I'm scared.

DEREEN: One,

FATU: two,

FARINAZ: three eternities pass.

YARVIN: The door opens. I see a big, white woman with a booming voice.

FATU: Will she like me?

FARINAZ: Will the beatings start again?

YARVIN: My foster mom, Ellen Gibson, says:

FARINAZ: "You have a family now. You're going to be just fine, and your baby is going to be just fine, too."

YARVIN: She hugs me really hard.

(All clap.)

FATU: 2000.

ALL: 2000.

FATU: I am taking a nap. Suddenly, my sister, Mary, says:

YARVIN: "Fatu! Fatu! Wake up! Come look!"

FATU: When I look out the window, I see something I have never seen before.

ALL: Snow!

FATU: We are so excited, we run outside without our winter coats or boots.

ABDUL: We taste the snow.

YARVIN: We feel the snow.

FATU: Then I get a bucket and fill it with snow. I want to save it and take it back to Sierra Leone one day to show my friends.

FATU AND ABDUL: 2000.

FARINAZ: 2000.

DEREEN: Poe Middle School.

FATU: On the first day of school I am surprised that nobody is wearing a uniform. I am surprised to see so many different kinds of kids. I have no friends. At first, I don't eat lunch because the food is so different here. It's no problem, I can go without food. I'm used to being hungry.

(All clap ten times. Blackout.
    Quiet, plaintive flute music begins to play in the background.
    Lights up. One by one, each performer presents a poem in his/her native language. These poems are not translated, but create a medley of different languages. The flute music plays throughout. After the concluding poem, Farinaz speaks:)

FARINAZ: You can choose anything in the world, my child, but you can never choose your heritage.

(All clap ten times.)

FATU: 2000.

ALL: 2000.

DEREEN: Poe Middle School.

FATU: I am in home-economics class. I make something called:

ALL: pizza.

FATU: But when I taste it, I hate it. I throw it in the garbage. I've never tasted cheese before.

(All clap.)

YARVIN: 2001.

ALL: 2001.

YARVIN: I am sent to see a therapist. I'm scared. I don't want to talk about the past. I don't want to feel the pain again. Later, the therapist says:

FARINAZ: "What happened to you is *not* your fault."

YARVIN: I don't need to be Melissa Coreas anymore. It was good to let the sadness out, to let the tears flow, to tell my story to someone else. For the first time in my life, I don't have to be afraid of bad things happening to me over and over again.

(All clap.)

FATU: 2001.

ALL: 2001.

FARINAZ: September 11, 2001.

FATU: In Sierra Leone, I know who to run to, where to run to, to protect myself. Here, neighbors don't know each other. I worry about people here. They aren't used to war; they don't know how to protect themselves. I will teach them how to crawl when the shooting starts.

(All clap.)

DEREEN: 2001.

ALL: 2001.

FARINAZ: September 11, 2001.

DEREEN: Several students ask me:

ABDUL: "Are you with Al-Qaeda?"

(All clap.)

2001.

ALL: 2001.

DEREEN: October 14, 2001.

ABDUL: We are on an airplane for the first time. I have my first cup of coffee. I can't sleep for three days! We fly to:

FARINAZ: Dubai,

YARVIN: London,

FARINAZ: New York.

(All clap.)

ABDUL AND FATU: 2001.

ALL: 2001.

FARINAZ: New York City.

ABDUL: At the hotel, I go through a revolving door. My little brother, Mashal, likes it so much he goes round and round, over and over again. Our first dinner in America is:

FATU: french fries,

YARVIN: Afghani-style chicken and

ALL: pizza.

ABDUL: In the hotel, there are apples. When I bite into one, I discover it is wood. We sleep in a bed for the first time. In Pakistan, we all slept on a rug.

(All clap.)

2001.

ALL: 2001.

FARINAZ: Holmes Middle School.

ABDUL: It is my first day of school. My teacher says:

FARINAZ: "We have a new child in class. He is from Afghanistan. Be nice to him."

ABDUL: There are so many different kinds of kids here, but I make friends quickly. I can talk to them about Jackie Chan, Michael Jackson and the big guy with all the muscles—

ALL: Arnold Schwarzenegger!

(All clap.)

FATU: 2001.

ALL: 2001.

FATU: I hear an airplane. I run to the closet and hide. My older sister says:

FARINAZ: "Fatu, Fatu, we are in the United States now, not in Sierra Leone."

FATU: I know I'm here, but my body doesn't believe it. It takes a long time for me to get over any sudden loud noise. I *still* have problems sleeping.

(All clap.)

FARINAZ: 2002.

ALL: 2002.

DEREEN: Falls Church, Virginia.

FARINAZ: In 2002, I receive a degree in counseling and join the Center for Multicultural Human Services, a mental health organization staffed largely by immigrants, for immigrants and refugees, both adults and children. I am working in a program specifically for survivors of torture and severe trauma. This includes not only victims of political wars, but also victims of urban and domestic wars.

(All clap.)

DEREEN: 2002.

ALL: 2002.

FATU: Centerville, Virginia.

DEREEN: In our townhouse every day from 5 P.M. to 7 P.M., I watch the Kurdish channel from Iraq with my mother, to stay in touch with my homeland. Then, I go upstairs to my room and watch *The Simpsons.*

(All clap.)

FATU: 2002.

ALL: 2002.

YARVIN: Annandale High School.

FATU: In world history class, we are watching a videotape about war. A student says:

DEREEN: "That's really horrible!"

YARVIN: "That's really nasty!"

FATU: I say:

FARINAZ: "That's not nasty. I've experienced worse than that!"

FATU: When I tell the students what I've seen, they don't believe me. I decide not to tell anyone any more of my experiences.

(All clap.)

YARVIN: 2002.

ALL: 2002.

YARVIN: My daughter, Emely, is now twenty-two months old. Every day before I leave her to go to school, I hug her and say:

FARINAZ: "I love you."

YARVIN: She will never have to suffer as I did, and I will never deny her a mother's love.

(All clap.)

FATU: 2002.
ALL: 2002.
FATU: I am invited to tell my story in a theater production called *Children of War*. Maybe this time, people will understand what I have been through. Maybe this time, they will believe me.

(All clap.)

ABDUL: 2002.
ALL: 2002.
ABDUL: My father is having a hard time. The language is hard for him. He still has nightmares about the war. My mom says:
FARINAZ: "I miss the comforts we had back home, like a cook and other help. We can't afford that here. I miss being a nurse, and I had wanted to become a doctor, but my children will get an education here. Abdul, when you grow up here in America you will have the chance to be a successful man."

(All clap.)

YARVIN: 2002.
ALL: 2002.
YARVIN: Three years have passed since I moved into my foster home. I am still there. I have a real family now. When I go to school, my foster mother takes care of my baby. José and I are still together. I have a new start and a new life in front of me. I want to study criminal justice, but the first thing I will do when I graduate from high school is work as a 911 dispatcher. I want to help other people.

(All clap.)

DEREEN: 2002.
ALL: 2002.
DEREEN: Freedom is precious to my people. The Kurdish people are the largest ethnic group in the world without a homeland, without freedom. But does anybody care about a powerless people? Will the United States care about the freedom of the Kurdish people? Only time will tell. For now, my family lives as refugees in another country. My mother says:

FARINAZ: "We must learn to fit in, to adjust, taking good things from back home and mixing them with the good things here."

DEREEN: I have made the adjustment to a new life here, but I wish that my father could be here with us now.

(All clap.)

FARINAZ: 2002.

ALL: 2002.

FARINAZ: It's been eleven years since I left Iran. I've been back once, in 1998. I have no desire to resettle there. My home is within me now. I am a citizen of the world now.

(All clap.)

2002.

ALL: 2002.

YARVIN: December 2002.

FARINAZ: On this evening, five children bear witness to their personal experiences of war. Abdul, Yarvin, Dereen and Fatu represent some of the children who have survived the harrowing experience of war. They are triumphant children. But there are many more who do not survive. Some children are so damaged by war that they will never grow up and live normal lives. Others are victims in the urban and suburban wars of domestic abuse, who speak at their own peril. The leading cause of children's deaths in the United States is at the hands of a parent, either through neglect or abuse. Finally, there are those children trapped in gangs who cannot speak for fear of reprisals and expulsion from school. In Northern Virginia, the schools have a zero-tolerance policy for gang involvement. These children, the children we have no names for, the children who cannot tell their stories are:

ALL: Invisible.

(All clap ten times.
An uplifting choral song begins to play softly in the background. It continues through the finale.)

YARVIN: My name is Yarvin. I was born in Llano los Patos, Department of Union, El Salvador on July 25, 1984. On the day I was born, my uncle Jorge went to America. It was summer.
Abdul?

(She closes her script and stands.)

ABDUL: My name is Abdul. I was born on October 12, 1989, in Kabul, Afghanistan, at 3:30 A.M. I was born two months premature. It was a cold winter night.
    Farinaz?

(He closes his script and stands.)

FARINAZ: My name is Farinaz. I was born on April 23, 1960, in Tehran, Iran, on a sunny day. I am the eldest of three children. It was spring.
    Fatu?

(She closes her script and stands.)

FATU: My name is Fatu. I was born in Freetown, Sierra Leone, on June 20, 1987. I am named for my grandmother. It was the rainy season.
    Dereen?

(She closes her script and stands.)

DEREEN: My name is Dereen. I am Kurdish. I was born in Sulaimaniya, Kurdistan, on January 17, 1987, at 3 A.M. On the day I was born, bombs fell on my city.

(Music up. The performers face the audience and repeat their gestures from the beginning of the performance: raising, crossing and lowering their arms slowly and gracefully in unison, as the lights fade to black.)

END

UE 92/06 (Anniversary Production)

A Special Commemorative Performance:
Lafayette College, Pennsylvania / 2006

Conceived and directed by Ping Chong
Written by Ping Chong and Talvin Wilks,
with Sara Zatz

IN COLLABORATION WITH:
Saul Alvina
Angel Gardner
Leyla Modirzadeh
Tania Salmen

In 2002, I celebrated my thirtieth anniversary as an independent artist and the tenth anniversary of the *Undesirable Elements* series. To commemorate these landmarks, we created an anniversary season at La MaMa E.T.C., which has been the home to so many of my works over the years. We decided to create a special *Undesirable Elements* anniversary production bringing together memorable cast members from productions around the country over the preceding ten years. I asked my collaborator Talvin Wilks to work with me putting together the script. To complete the circle, I decided to join the cast myself for the first time. Since the theme of "Otherness" and the role of the outsider is so central to all my work, it seemed like a no-brainer. Like the very first *Undesirable Elements*, the anniversary production, originally titled *UE 92/02*, had an unexpected ongoing life. First, we were invited to bring it to Lille, France, for the Lille European Capital of Culture Celebration; then to Italy for the RomaEuropa Festival; then to the Colorado Festival of World Theatre; and, most recently, to the Williams Center for the Arts in Pennsylvania, which is the version included here. As a touring piece with cast members from all over the United States, it was able to transcend the local nature of regular *Undesirable Elements* pieces and speak to something larger in the ever-changing question: "What does it mean to be American?" As the production toured and some of the original anniversary cast members were no longer available, we brought in other "all-stars" to join in. I enjoyed being a cast member in the anniversary production, as it allowed me to see how the other half lives, so to speak, and how hard the casts work to achieve the unique rhythms of the script. Not to mention the endless teasing I received from my fellow cast mates, if I occasionally missed a line or a clap during performance!

—*Ping Chong*

PRODUCTION HISTORY

UE 92/06 premiered at the Williams Center for the Arts at Lafayette College in Easton, Pennsylvania, on November 14, 2006. It was conceived and directed by Ping Chong. It was written by Ping Chong and Talvin Wilks, with Sara Zatz, in collaboration with the cast. The performers were Saul Avina (*Undesirable Elements/Atlanta, 2001*), Ping Chong, Angel Gardner (*Undesirable Elements/New York, 1993*), Leyla Modirzadeh (*Undesirable Elements/Seattle, 1995*) and Tania Salmen (*Original Production, Undesirable Elements, 1992; Undesirable Elements/New York, 1993; Secret History, 2000*). The lighting designer was Darren McCroom and the stage manager was Courtney Golden. The managing director was Bruce Allardice and the project manager was Sara Zatz.

UE 92/06 was produced with support from The Nathan Cummings Foundation, the National Endowment for the Arts, New York State Council on the Arts, New York City Department of Cultural Affairs, The Andrew W. Mellon Foundation and MetLife Foundation.

Five music stands and chairs stand upstage, arranged in a curve, around a white semicircle. Each music stand holds a copy of the script, which the performers read from throughout the performance. None of the performers ever leaves the stage.

Lights slowly come up. A haunting Norwegian incantation plays. One at a time, the performers approach their music stand. One by one, they turn to face the audience. As the incantation plays, the performers face the audience and slowly, ritually, raise their arms to the side, then bring them forward, crossing them in front of their bodies, then open them out again, and bring them down to their sides. This motion is repeated slowly and gracefully in unison, as if they are moving through water. The incantation fades out at the end of the gestures.

LEYLA: بیا شروع کنیم

SAUL: *Vamos a comenzar.*

TANIA: يلا بلشنا

PING: 現在開始上課

ANGEL (*Translating for all*): Let's get started. Please sit.

(The ensemble sits in their chairs.)

LEYLA: من لیلا مدیرزاده هستم. و 02 ژوئیه 1967 ساعت 5:03 بعدازظهر در دور هام، کارولینای شمالی بهدنیا آمدهام. پزشکی که من را به دنیا آورد به مادرم گفت "زودباش! میخوام برم خونه شام بخورم." تابستان خیلی خوبی بود. Saul؟

71

SAUL: *Mi nombre es Saul Alejandro Avina. Nací 18 de septiembre de 1978 en la Ciudad de México. Nací durante la semana del Día de la Independencia. Soy el más joven de tres hermanos.*

Tania?

TANIA: اسمي تانيا سلمان. خلقت باليوم التاني بتشرين التاني، ألف وتسعمية وتلاتة وستين بمهرتين، فنزويلا، بيوم الميت. حصان اسمه تانيا ربح السباق هاليوم Ping؟

PING: 我姓張名平，壹千九百四十六年秋天十月二號加拿大多倫多世。

Angel?

ANGEL: My name is Angela Beth Gardner. I was born on January 20, 1966, in New York City, USA. It must have been winter.

(All clap.)

Jonathan.

SAUL: Diego.

PING: Jean Yu.

TANIA: Hamed.

LEYLA: Nakissa.

ANGEL: Mark.

SAUL: Manuel.

PING: Yee Han.

TANIA: Yasin.

LEYLA: Erfan.

ANGEL: Sarah.

SAUL: Cuahutemec.

PING: Bak Lin.

TANIA: Ishaq.

LEYLA: Parisa.

ANGEL: Noah.

SAUL: Tititochtli.

PING: Sui Long.

TANIA: Wafiq.

LEYLA: Royya.

ANGEL: Menno.

SAUL: Ernesto.

PING: Seal Juk.

TANIA: Aida.

LEYLA: Mehdi.

ANGEL: Rachel.

SAUL: Juan.

PING: Fei Fei.

TANIA: Abdalla.

LEYLA: Tahere.

(All clap ten times.)

TANIA: Indigenous Mexican names and their meanings:
SAUL: Xochiyotl,
ANGEL: meaning "heart of a gentle flower."
SAUL: Tlanexic,
LEYLA: meaning "light of dawn."
SAUL: Yolihuani,
PING: meaning "source of life."
SAUL: Tepiltzin,
TANIA: meaning "priveleged son."
SAUL: Xochiquetzal,
ANGEL: meaning "most beautiful flower."
SAUL: Xicohtencatl,
PING: meaning
ALL: "angry bumblebee."

(All clap.)

ANGEL: In Leyla's family, all of the children are named after Persian
    poets or poetic figures:
LEYLA: Khayyam,
ANGEL: after Omar Khayyam.
LEYLA: Hafez,
ANGEL: after the great Persian poet Hafez, who wrote *The Book of Life*.
LEYLA: Leyla,
ANGEL: after the famous love poem "Leyli and Majnun," in which
    Majnun goes crazy for the love of Leyli.

(All clap.)

PING: Lie Ping,
ALL: meaning
ANGEL: "beautiful harmony."
PING: Gum Ping,
ALL: meaning
SAUL: "golden harmony."
PING: Geen Ping,
ALL: meaning
TANIA: "harmonious health."

PING: Gar Ping,

ALL: meaning

LEYLA: "harmony in the family."

PING: Fung Ping,

ALL: meaning

ANGEL: "a phoenix of harmony."

PING: Gee Ping,

ALL: meaning

TANIA: "united harmony."

PING: All of my siblings have *Ping* as part of their names, which means "harmony and equality." My father wanted to stress that his male and female children were harmoniously equal.

(All clap.)

ANGEL: Lebanese names and nicknames:

TANIA: Ahmad, Mouhamad—

ALL: name.

TANIA: Hamoude—

ALL: nickname.

TANIA: Fayruz, Fida—

ALL: name.

TANIA: FouFou—

ALL: nickname.

TANIA: Jamal, Joumana—

ALL: name.

TANIA: Joujou—

ALL: nickname.

TANIA: Samir, Said—

ALL: name.

TANIA: SouSou—

ALL: nickname.

TANIA: Shadia, Shiraz—

ALL: name.

TANIA: ChouChou—

ALL: nickname.

(All clap.)

LEYLA: Italian?

PING: Middle-Eastern?

TANIA: African-American?

SAUL: Latina?

LEYLA: Haitian?

PING: Jamaican.

TANIA: Sudanese!

ANGEL: The guy at Lofty's Couscous in the Village swore I was

ALL: Moroccan!

ANGEL: Every day, people speak Spanish to me on the street and assume I know what they are saying. People never assume I'm an African-American Jew who was born in New York City and raised by white, middle-class Mennonites in Northern Indiana. Some of my friends assume that I'm only interested in the latest film by Spike Lee, the latest book by Toni Morrison, while other friends say:

PING: "I don't think of you as black."

ANGEL: Do they assume that's a compliment? People who know me assume.

> (*All clap ten times. Blackout.*
> *Beat.*
> *Lights up.*)

1620.

ALL: 1620.

ANGEL: The Mayflower lands on Plymouth Rock, bringing the first of my adoptive father's ancestors to this country. My father's roots can be traced to a wealthy slave owner in New Jersey named

LEYLA: Old Prince George van Nest.

PING: 1848.

ANGEL: 1848.

PING: Gold is discovered in California.

LEYLA: Many Chinese seeking their fortune become forty-niners.

TANIA: The Chinese are the first Asian immigrants.

SAUL: 1851.

ALL: 1851.

SAUL: The Mexican-American War.

ANGEL: A declaration by General Sam Houston:

LEYLA: "The Anglo-Saxon race must pervade the whole southern extremity of this vast continent. The Mexicans are no better than the Indians. I see no reason why we should not take their land."

SAUL: Mexico loses the war:

ANGEL: Texas,

TANIA: Arizona,

LEYLA: Utah,

PING: Colorado,

LEYLA: New Mexico,

ANGEL: California,

SAUL: all become part of the United States.

PING: 1852.

TANIA: 1852.

PING: The Governor of California:

ANGEL: "Let us encourage a further immigration and settlement of *the Chinese*—they are peculiar, but who isn't?"

PING: 1852.

TANIA: 1852.

PING: The Governor of California four months later:

ANGEL: "The Chinese are cunning and deceitful, they can never become like us and they are not of a race or native character which will ever elevate the social condition of California."

TANIA: 1860.

PING: 1860.

LEYLA: The country of Lebanon.

TANIA: The Druze, a religion and a people descended from Islam, rule Lebanon. Conflicts between Druze and Christians that go back hundreds of years boil over again. The French intervene in the guise of humanitarian mediation.

LEYLA *(In French)*: *Qui continuera a gouvèrner le Liban?*

TANIA *(Translating)*: Who will continue to rule Lebanon?

PING: 1869.

LEYLA: 1869.

SAUL: May 10, 1869.

PING: A commemorative photograph is taken when the Central Pacific Railroad meets the Union Pacific Railroad in Utah. Even though they represent ninety percent of the workforce of the Central Pacific, ten thousand Chinese-American pioneers are excluded from the photograph.

PING: 1869.

ANGEL: 1869.

PING: Meanwhile, down in Mississippi.

ALL: M-I-S-S-I-S-S-I-P-P-I.

PING: A decree:

LEYLA: "Emancipation has spoiled the Negro and carried him away from his place in the fields of agriculture. We, therefore, say let the coolies come, let them pick our cotton, let them work our fields, but they must become Christians, of course."

ALL: Of course, of course, of course.

LEYLA: "We did not let the Indian stand in the way of civilization, so why let the Chinese barbarians? I suggest we do to them as we have done to the Indian—"

ALL: "Put them on reservations."

PING: 1882.

TANIA: 1882.

PING: The Chinese Exclusion Act—

ANGEL: the first immigrant law to exclude on the basis of race:

LEYLA: "Hereafter, no state or federal court of the United States shall admit Chinese to citizenship."

ANGEL: 1886.

SAUL: 1886.

ANGEL: Fleeing religious persecution because of their refusal to support the draft, Caroline Lehman's Mennonite parents emigrate from Berne, Switzerland, to Berne, Indiana. Caroline will grow up and marry Emil Fleuckiger, another Swiss Mennonite immigrant, and they will raise ten children on the flat farmland of Indiana.

PING: 1913.

ANGEL AND LEYLA: 1913.

TANIA: Foshan, China.

PING: An earnest boy named Jean Yu begs his grandmother on his knees to be allowed to go to school. Literacy is not a given in China, it is a privilege few can afford. Jean Yu's family is not poor, but his father is the black sheep of the family. Nevertheless, his grandmother agrees to let him go. He is ten years old.

(All clap.)

TANIA: 1920.

ANGEL: 1920.

ALL: 1920.

TANIA: France officially "occupies" Lebanon.

LEYLA: Read: "colonize."

TANIA: The Muslim population is heavily taxed to the advantage of Christians.

PING: Read: "discrimination."

TANIA: The French say:

LEYLA (In French): "Nous sommes ici pour libérer les Chrétiens de la domination Musulmane."

TANIA (*Translating*): "We are here to liberate Christians from Muslim domination."

PING: 1922.

ANGEL: 1922.

LEYLA: Guangzhou, China.

PING: A young girl named Bak Lin joins the Chinese Opera. She kneels before her master and offers him a cup of dark tea.

SAUL: There will be no talking back,

TANIA: no misbehaving.

ANGEL: If the master wants you to stand on your head, you stand on your head.

LEYLA: If the master wants you to sweep the rehearsal space, you sweep the rehearsal space.

PING: It is a lesson in humility. On break, Bak Lin ingratiates herself to the musicians by filling their opium pipes. They will teach this clever child many things.

LEYLA: 1928.

PING AND ANGEL: 1928.

TANIA: New York City.

LEYLA: My grandmother marries Ernest Quilter, a sculptor from South Africa—a Russian Jew marrying an Irish Catholic. Years later she would divorce him, saying:

ANGEL: "I just couldn't afford him anymore!"

TANIA: 1929.

SAUL: 1929.

LEYLA: Shwaifet, Lebanon.

TANIA: A young man arrives with a chaperone at Bahia's house. She, her sister, and female cousins shove each other aside to see the tall, handsome stranger on the other side of the keyhole.

LEYLA: Who is he?

SAUL: What's he doing here?

ANGEL: Whose hand in marriage is he asking for?

TANIA: 1929.

LEYLA: 1929.

ANGEL: Shwaifet, Lebanon.

TANIA: The wedding.

ALL: One.

TANIA: The bride sits on a throne surrounded by flowers in her mother's house.

ALL: Two.

LEYLA: The men of both families are dancing together in one room and the women are dancing together in another room.

ALL: Three.

PING: *Jileb* is served—

TANIA: a drink made of dates, chopped nuts and ice.

ALL: Four.

ANGEL: *Mezza* is served—

TANIA: a selection of small savory dishes.

ALL: Five.

PING: Then both families go to the groom's house and the party starts all over again.

ALL: Six.

LEYLA: After the guests are gone, the newlyweds are brought to the bridal chamber.

ALL: Seven.

ANGEL: Then they are put into a special bridal blanket, like a huge pocket, which is tied on the outside for the night.

ALL: Eight.

TANIA: The next morning, everyone comes to congratulate the newlyweds and a huge breakfast is served. *(Beat)* Foua'd and Bahia, Bahia and Foua'd. These two young people will become my grandparents.

(All clap.)

SAUL: 1930.

ALL: 1930.

SAUL: In the 1920 U.S. census, Mexican Americans were counted as whites. In the 1930 census, Mexican Americans are reassigned to a racial category separate from whites.

ALL: Who decides?

PING: 1934.

LEYLA: 1934.

ANGEL: San Francisco, California.

PING: Fates converge. Bak Lin, the diva, meets Jean Yu, the director/librettist. They are working in the same opera company entertaining the homesick Chinese in a hostile America. They will become my parents.

(All clap.)

LEYLA: 1939.

PING: 1939.

ANGEL: Tehran, Iran.

LEYLA: Javad Modirzadeh marries Saquineh. She is nine; he is fifteen. She has her first of five children when she is thirteen. She will become my grandmother.

(All clap.)

TANIA: 1940.

ALL: 1940.

PING: World War II.

TANIA: On top of exploiting the Lebanese people, the French draft the men to fight their war against Germany. My grandfather flees to Libya. His brother flees to Malta.

LEYLA: Family upon family is torn apart.

PING: Some stay and resist the French.

TANIA: 1941.

SAUL AND LEYLA: 1941.

ANGEL: November 26, 1941.

TANIA: As a result of national and international pressure, France proclaims the independence of Lebanon. However, like all puppet masters, they continue to pull the strings behind the scenes.

PING: 1941.

LEYLA: 1941.

SAUL: Hong Kong.

PING: Jean Yu and Bak Lin throw in their lot to make a life together in the New World, but having two young children and trying to make a living in the opera is too difficult. My parents leave my two sisters with my aunts to raise them in Hong Kong. Then they return to America by ship. Midway across the Pacific, there is a great commotion among the Chinese passengers. The Japanese have attacked Hong Kong. My parents lose all contact with my sisters.

PING: 1941.

TANIA: 1941.

LEYLA AND ANGEL: 1941.

ALL: 1941.

PING: A sea of terrified people carrying what they can, in whatever way they can, march out of Hong Kong by foot toward Guangzhou Province. Within this chaotic mass of humanity, my sisters are carried in woven baskets suspended on a bamboo pole. They are two and three years old.

(All clap.)

1943.

LEYLA: 1943.

TANIA: Guangzhou, China.

PING: Hunger.

LEYLA: There is too much hunger.

ANGEL: There is prolonged hunger.

PING: My sisters eat peanut or tofu dregs, stuff usually fed to pigs. Sometimes it is possible to get innards because the Japanese won't eat them. When my aunts take my sisters to my grandfather's house, desperate for food, he refuses to open the door. By depositing my sisters with my mother's family instead of his, my father has committed a serious breach of etiquette.

PING: 1943.

TANIA: 1943.

LEYLA: Meanwhile, in Vancouver, Canada.

PING: There is no work in the Chinese opera. A diva and an opera director, not used to hard physical labor, find themselves picking potatoes on a farm. They subsist on rice porridge and worm-eaten dried fish. A son is born, but my parents are too poor to keep him. He is given to another Chinese family. My parents still do not know if their two daughters are dead or alive in China.

TANIA: 1945.

SAUL: 1945.

TANIA: The French rulers of Lebanon say:

LEYLA *(In French)*: *"Les Arabes ne sont pas suffisament civilisés pour se gouverner."*

TANIA *(Translating)*: "Arabs are not civilized enough to rule themselves."

ANGEL: But the Lebanese say:

TANIA *(In Arabic)*: ‏"المهتل ما بيهتل منا".‏

ALL *(Translating)*: "Those taking care of us are not taking care of us."

PING: 1945.

ANGEL: 1945.

LEYLA AND TANIA: 1945.

PING: Dysentery.

SAUL: Cholera.

LEYLA: Bodies wrapped in woven mats on wooden carts,

TANIA: burnt-out rubble,

ANGEL: bombs exploding,

LEYLA: flies buzzing everywhere,

TANIA: the stench of death—

PING: these are the things of daily life in war-torn China. My uncle grows sick and dies when a young diva, hiding from the Japanese, is caught and bayoneted to death in front of him. My aunt and sisters, now utterly alone, are reduced to sheltering in the corner of a roofless house. They make one last attempt to reach my father. They succeed.

ANGEL: 1945.

TANIA: 1945.

ANGEL: The end of World War II reveals to the world the systematic destruction of six million Jews. In America, in the South, signs read:

ALL: "No Coloreds Allowed."

TANIA: 1946.

ALL: 1946.

TANIA (*In Arabic*): الفرانس أخيراً تركوا لبنان.

ALL (*Translating*): The French finally leave Lebanon.

> (*Tania ululates; a joyous victory cry.*
>   *All clap ten times.*)

LEYLA (*In Farsi*): لطفا بایستید

> (*All rise. They change seats, walking single file around the outer perimeter of the semi-circle as the Norwegian incantation is repeated.*)

> (*In Farsi*) لطفا بنشینید

> (*All sit and open their scripts.*)

TANIA: 1947.

SAUL: 1947.

ANGEL: 1947.

ALL: 1947.

PING: Beirut, Lebanon.

TANIA (*Calling out an Arabic ice-cream vendor cry*): "Yaaa bouzaaa! Haleeb . . ."

ALL: "Yaaa bouzaaa! Haleeb . . ."

TANIA: From age six to fourteen, Mounir helps his mother sell ice cream—one flavor per day.

(All clap.)

1948.

ALL: 1948.

TANIA: With an aunt and two cousins, Mounir goes to join his father in Venezuela. His ice-cream-making days are over. They are in search of a better life. He will become my father.

(All clap.)

PING: 1950.

TANIA: 1950.

ANGEL: New York City.

LEYLA: There is no work in the Chinese Opera.

PING: My father now has seven mouths to feed—

ANGEL: not to mention his first wife from an arranged marriage and her two children,

PING: plus my uncle, who never seems to be able to make ends meet,

LEYLA: and his brood, still living in Hong Kong.

PING: All told,

ALL: twenty-one people.

PING: Being the oldest brother, it is his responsibility to support whoever needs to be supported. What can he do?

PING: 1950.

LEYLA: 1950.

PING: My two sisters return to the United States from China after nine years. They are held for three days at Ellis Island. When meals are served, they are announced with the clanging of a metal triangle. The first English word my sister Betty learns is:

ALL: "tea."

(All clap.)

PING: 1953.

ALL: 1953.

ANGEL: Chinatown. Bayard Street.

PING: At this time, Chinatown is bordered by the Bowery—lined with flophouses and saloons complete with brass spittoons— and to the north, Canal Street and Little Italy. These are the boundaries of my world. If I want to get beat up, all I have to do is cross Canal Street, and often I don't even have to do that.

(All clap.)

ANGEL: 1958.

ALL: 1958.

ANGEL: Merritt Post Gardner, a conscientious objector from New York City, and Ruth Ann Liechty, the granddaughter of Caroline Lehman from Berne, Indiana, sign up with the Mennonite Central Committee to be teachers for two years in rural Newfoundland. They are posted one hundred and twenty-five miles apart: he in St. Anthony Byte, she on Twillingate Island. It's a long distance by dog sled, but that doesn't stop the courtship. One December, Merritt hitches a ride in the back of a mail plane to be with Ruth Ann for Christmas. They will become my adoptive parents.

(All clap.)

TANIA: 1959.

LEYLA: 1959.

SAUL: Venezuela.

TANIA: My father is getting ready to visit Lebanon with his parents to search for a bride. Before leaving for the trip, he and his father have coffee at his uncle's store. A VW Bug drives up and a beautiful girl walks in. My father asks:

SAUL: "Who's that beautiful young lady?"

ANGEL: "That's my oldest daughter, Gledys."

TANIA: My father cancels his trip to Lebanon. If the VW Bug hadn't pulled up that day, I would not be here now.

(All clap.)

PING: 1960.

LEYLA: 1960.

TANIA: Little Italy.

PING: I cross the Canal Street border out of Chinatown carefully to go to junior high in Little Italy. Half of the kids are Italian and half are Chinese. Once I get to know the Italian kids, it's okay. In my class, there is a Welsh kid who keeps getting beaten up by the Italian kids because he speaks standard American English. Despite the warnings of the Chinese community—

ANGEL: "Don't trust white people. They'll screw you."

PING: —he becomes my first white friend.

LEYLA: 1960.

ALL: 1960.

ANGEL: Durham, North Carolina.

LEYLA: Joan Quilter leaves New York City to go to graduate school at Duke University. She studies French, but she really wants to be an international spy. At a tea for foreign students, she meets Jamal Modirzadeh, a very stylish, ambitious medical student. He is from Iran. She says he looks like Clark Gable. If they had not met that night, I would not be here now.

(All clap.)

PING: 1960.

ALL: 1960.

PING: It's time to decide which high school to go to. Since I'm no good in science or math or anything else except art, I choose the High School of Art and Design. When I tell my art teacher, she says:

ANGEL: "Do you know who Titian is?"

LEYLA: "Raphael?"

TANIA: "Michelangelo?"

SAUL: "Leonardo da Vinci?"

PING: I say:

TANIA: "No, I don't."

PING: I can hear the contempt in her voice:

ANGEL: "How can this ignorant Asian boy go to an art school?"

PING: 1960.

SAUL: 1960.

PING: I leave my Chinese village to go to the High School of Art and Design, all the way uptown on 57th Street and 2nd Avenue. I have to take a subway to get there. It's another planet:

LEYLA: Tiffany's,

SAUL: Carnegie Hall,

TANIA: Saks Fifth Avenue,

ANGEL: movie stars walking their poodles.

PING: When I get to Art and Design, I find that I am the only Asian student in a school of five hundred.

ANGEL: 1965.

LEYLA AND TANIA: 1965.

ANGEL: Merrit Gardner, now living in Pennsylvania with his wife Ruth Ann, reads an article in the *Saturday Evening Post*. He is inspired by a surprising statistic:

PING: "For every white orphaned baby there are twenty families waiting to adopt. For every twenty black orphaned babies there is
only one family waiting to adopt."

ANGEL: Already with two sons, Merrit convinces Ruth Ann that this
might be a good way to add to their family.

(All clap.)

PING: 1965.

ALL: 1965.

PING: I remember it very well. My mother was wearing very, very red
lipstick. There was a dainty curl of hair symmetrically placed
on each side of her forehead. She was wearing a heavy, dark
mink coat that was cold to the touch. It must have been winter.
(Beat) I remember it very well. My mother was wailing inconsol-
ably. She was drunk and she was reeling and she was not to be
comforted. She was wailing for the son she had to give away in
Vancouver, Canada, so many years ago. She was wailing for her
son, my immediate brother, whom I have never met.

ANGEL: 1965.

ALL: 1965.

ANGEL: A Catholic agency that the Gardner's had contacted about a
transracial adoption responds:

LEYLA: "No, dearie, we're not up in those clouds yet."

ANGEL: Eventually they contact the Louise Wise Services in New
York City, a Jewish organization providing adoptions for Jewish
and biracial children.

PING: 1965.

TANIA: 1965.

SAUL: 1965.

PING: Miracle of miracles! The racist immigration laws of the United
States, which favored Europeans, are finally changed. This will
alter the face of America.

(All clap.)

1965.

SAUL AND ANGEL: 1965.

TANIA: July 29, 1965.

PING: The burden of supporting twenty-one people finally kills my
poor father. Just before he dies, my father, who had to beg on
his knees to go to school, says to me:

ANGEL: "Really apply yourself and study hard in school."

PING: I do not have a chance to connect with him as an adult before he leaves me. I am just beginning to spread my wings, impatient to leave the nest. I feel myself increasingly moving away from my culture—his world—and into a new one. It is like the expulsion from Eden, from belonging—except it is by choice.

ANGEL: 1966.

ALL: 1966.

TANIA: New York City.

ANGEL: A nineteen-year-old, single Jewish girl relinquishes her newborn for adoption. The baby girl is biracial. Four weeks later, Merrit and Ruth Ann Gardner bring me home.

(All clap.)

1967.

LEYLA: 1967.

PING: February 21, 1967.

ANGEL: I am one year old. My parents appear on TV on *The David Susskind Show*. The topic is transracial adoption. During a question and answer period, some African-American audience members accuse them of:

TANIA: "brainwashing black children into the white world."

(All clap.)

ANGEL: 1969.

ALL: 1969.

ANGEL: My father gets a tenured position as a math professor at a Mennonite college in Indiana. We move to the all-white community of Goshen. I am three years old.

(All clap.)

PING: 1970.

ALL: 1970.

PING: I graduate from film school but I don't know what to do. I decide to take dance classes at New York University with the *enfant terrible* of the avant-garde dance scene, Meredith Monk. The rest of the students are there to lose weight. At the end of the course, Meredith says:

LEYLA: "I like the way you move. Come to my workshop."

PING: "Okay." But I don't go.

ANGEL: 1970.

ALL: 1970.

ANGEL: My parents celebrate my blackness. They buy me a brown-skinned, brown-eyed doll with a little kinky afro, just like mine. They make sure we have black babysitters. They read us storybooks that illustrate children every color of the rainbow. And on my wall, in black and white, a large poster of a little girl who looks just like me, naked as the day she was born, with the words:

ALL: "Black Is Beautiful!"

ANGEL: In the Jewish tradition, lineage is passed down from the mother. So, technically I'm Jewish, but my parents don't talk about that.

LEYLA: 1970.

SAUL: 1970.

LEYLA: We move to France so my mother can finish her thesis. At a local kindergarten, I watch as a group of children surround a little gypsy girl and tear out her hair. Tufts of dark hair float up into the wind. Two days later, I see her almost bald. Since I resemble the little gypsy girl, I only make friends with children who have blond or red hair. I do not want to become an

ALL: UNDESIRABLE ELEMENT.

(All clap.)

PING: 1970.

TANIA: 1970.

PING: I don't know what to do. I'm a slacker, "slackering" all over the place. One day I'm crossing Houston Street off Broadway and I run into Meredith Monk:

LEYLA: "Why didn't you come to my workshop? I've got one tonight. It's right across the street. It's at eight. Come."

PING: I'm too shy and too nervous to go. I walk around the block four times, then I screw up the courage. If I had not climbed up those stairs into Meredith's loft that day, I would not be here now.

(All clap ten times. Blackout.
Lights come back up and, one by one, each performer sings a song in his/her native language in the following order: Leyla, Tania, Saul, Ping. These songs are not translated, but create a medley of different languages.
Angel is last. She sings the first verse of a Mennonite hymn alone.)

ANGEL:

> Praise God from whom all blessings flow,
> Praise Him all creatures here below,
> Praise Him above, ye Heavenly Hosts,
> Praise Father, Son and Holy Ghost.

(*The ensemble repeats the verse in chorus.*
Beat.)

TANIA: Ping?

PING: Yes, Tania?

TANIA: What do you think of when I say the word "China"?

PING: I think of the classic Chinese novel *Romance of the Three Kingdoms*, with the opening line:

LEYLA: "Kingdoms wax and wane."

PING: I think of the word *yan*,

ANGEL: meaning "to endure suffering,"

PING: that so characterizes the lives of the Chinese people. I think of a white snake turning into a beautiful woman, a monkey king stealing the peaches of immortality from Heaven. I think of Chinese home cooking:

LEYLA: summer melon braised with dried scallops,

ANGEL: dried salted fish, pan-fried with garlic, sugar and vinegar,

TANIA: Chinese bacon steamed with dried shrimps or dried olives.

PING: I think of eating well with lots of people at a round table, regardless of race or color.

SAUL: Angel?

ANGEL: Yes, Saul?

SAUL: What do you think of when I say the words "African American"?

ANGEL: I think of a man who gave me life whom I have never met.

LEYLA: Angel, what do you think of when I say the word "Indiana"?

ANGEL: I think of Goshen, the town I grew up in: flat landscapes, cornfields, industrial parks, little black boy lawn-jockey ornaments. I think of being an outsider in my own community.

TANIA: What do you think of when I say the word "Mennonite"?

ANGEL: I think of Anabaptists, those who have been "baptized again." I think of singing hymns in four-part harmony. I think of Pennsylvania Dutch cooking: scrapple, headcheese and homemade applesauce. I think of belonging to a community of outsiders.

PING: Angel, what do you think of when I say the word "Jewish"?

ANGEL: I think of a woman who gave me life whom I've never met.
SAUL: What do you think of when I say the word "Mexico"?
ALL: Aztec Indians.
SAUL: I think of the extermination of the native peoples of Mexico.
ALL: Wetbacks.
SAUL: I think of humans being trapped in a stereotype.
ALL: Illegal aliens.
SAUL: People doing the jobs that nobody wants.
ALL: Migrant workers.
SAUL: The backbone of American agriculture.
ALL: Cancun.
SAUL: I think of the invisibility of my people as they serve margaritas to tourists.
ALL: Taco Bell.
SAUL: I think of ignorance.
TANIA: Leyla?
LEYLA: Yes, Tania?
TANIA: What do you think of when I say the word "Iran"?
LEYLA: I think of *fesunjun*,
PING: a chicken dish made with crushed walnuts and pomegranates.
LEYLA: The saltiest pistachios and the sweetest apricots. Salt on watermelons and lettuce dipped in honey. Rose petal jam, rose ice cream, rose water by the sink for hands. Persian poetry and the music of the *ney*,
TANIA: a flute blown from between your upper lip and teeth.
LEYLA: Sucking strong tea through a cube of sugar held in my mouth until it disintegrates. I think of my father singing in the shower, sounding like the call to prayer.
TANIA: What do you think of when I say the word "Lebanon"?
LEYLA: Long architectural noses.
ANGEL: Very sweet desserts.
SAUL: The cedars of Lebanon.
PING: Greek and Roman ruins.
ANGEL: Tania?
TANIA: Yes, Angel?
ANGEL: What do *you* think of when I say the word "Lebanon"?
TANIA: I think of my bomb pieces and bullet collection. My only doll, Patatina. *Allah*, everywhere. Walking in a pine forest picking pine nuts. Going to buy fresh milk from Bedouin tents early in the morning. Im-Ali, our Egyptian maid, teaching me belly dancing. Eating *baida ou sawda*, which is raw liver and fat. *(Singing)* "Ya Leli, ya aini," reading the future in coffee grounds. Singing

while eating, eating while singing, clapping and dancing—the whole family together, all my friends together doing this:

(Tania comes center stage and belly dances to lively Lebanese pop music.)

I think of the silence of the dead.

(We hear the tolling of six bells.)

PING *(In Chinese)*: 请站起来

(All rise. They change seats, walking single file around the outer perimeter of the semi- circle as the Norwegian incantation is repeated.)

请坐

(All sit and open their scripts.)

ANGEL: 1972.
SAUL: 1972.
LEYLA: 1972.
ALL: 1972.
TANIA: Goshen, Indiana.
ANGEL: My best friend, Debbie Miller, and I are playing beauty parlor. When it comes time to do my hair, Debbie tries her best to comb mine down flat. I remember her saying:
LEYLA: "If you comb it long enough like this, some day it will be straight."
ANGEL: I am eight years old.

(All clap.)

PING: 1972.
SAUL: 1972.
ALL: 1972.
PING: Meredith Monk has asked me to join her dance company. But even as I embrace the larger white world, my sense of alienation grows. I am in it, but I don't belong to it. The need to express this sense of Otherness gives birth to my first independent theater work—ironically entitled *Lazarus*, the biblical story of a man who comes back from the dead. A man who is utterly alone

in his knowledge of the other world, a knowledge that cannot be expressed in the world he has returned to.

LEYLA: 1973.

ALL: 1973.

LEYLA: After three years in France, my family moves to Iran. When we arrive in Tehran at night, the city looks like a jewel made of lights, but in the morning it looks like it's half built. My mother and brother Khayaam cannot assimilate into the life in Tehran. For my other brother Hafez and me, the city is magical. I am six years old.

(All clap.)

1974.

ANGEL: 1974.

PING: 1974.

TANIA: Tehran.

LEYLA: My parents' marriage becomes more and more troubled. When my mother walks down the street in a miniskirt, construction men throw rocks at her. My father doesn't understand why my mother won't follow the Iranian way of life. Finally, she leaves with her children. We have no place to go, so we end up living with my father's brother, Mahmoud, in San José, California. My mother, a single mom with a doctorate in French poetry, goes on welfare and changes the family name from Modirzadeh to Modir.

TANIA: 1975.

ALL: 1975.

TANIA: A normal day in Beirut. I am in my French reading class.

All of a sudden we hear a huge explosion. All the windows in the classroom shatter. The nuns take us down to the basement, which we have never seen before. They don't tell us what is going on; they just tell us to pray.

ALL (*Bowing heads, they place their palms together in prayer, and recite the Hail Mary prayer in French*):
  Je Vous Salue Marie.
  Je vous salue, Marie, pleine de grâce.
  Le Seigneur est avec vous.
  Vous êtes bénie entre toutes les femmes,
  et Jésus, le fruit de vos entrailles, est béni.

Sainte Marie, Mère de Dieu,
priez pour nous, pauvres pécheurs,
maintenant et à l'heure de notre mort.
Amen.

TANIA: My mother and my friend Joumana's father come to pick us up at the school. We are waiting at the door for them. Joumana's father is shot and killed right in front of our eyes. The complex war in Lebanon has begun.

(All clap.)

1975.

PING: 1975.

LEYLA: 1975.

SAUL: Beirut, Lebanon.

TANIA: The war is raging outside. Bombs whistle by our building. There are explosions everywhere. For three months, we are trapped with a limited food supply. We live in the foyer of our apartment because there are no windows there. One day, I am going to the bathroom. There are two bathrooms in the apartment, one on each end. Just as I flush the toilet, a bomb explodes down the hall. If I had gone to the other bathroom, I wouldn't be here now.

(All clap.)

1976.

ANGEL: 1976.

LEYLA AND PING: 1976.

TANIA: The war rages on. My father manages to get plane tickets for us to leave Lebanon. He asks us *(In Arabic),* ‏"وين بدكون تروحوا؟
على الولايات المتحدة، على السعودية، أو على فنزويلا؟"

LEYLA *(Translating)*: "Where do you want to go? The United States, Saudi Arabia or Venezuela?"

ALL: Venezuela!

(All clap.)

PING: 1978.

ALL: 1978.

PING: From 1972 to 1978, I'm on tour with Meredith Monk. In Venice, Florence and Milan, I finally see the works of Titian,

Raphael, Michelangelo and Leonardo da Vinci. It suddenly dawns on me that, of all the siblings, I am the one to follow in my parents' artistic footsteps. But I feel as if I am in a parallel universe from them, from my roots. I see and feel them, but they are on the other side of a glass wall. I want my culture back in my life, but I don't know how to cross the threshold. I don't know where the door is.

LEYLA: 1979.

ANGEL: 1979.

PING: 1979.

SAUL: San José, California.

LEYLA: The Iranian revolution begins. Khomeini seizes power as the shah falls. Suddenly, everyone knows where Iran is. What they don't know is that the United States' support of the shah helped to create the situation that put Khomeini into power. I see the first anti-Iranian bumper stickers:

ANGEL: "Bomb Iran!"

PING: "The Ayatollah is an Assahola!"

LEYLA: I see a sign in a restaurant that says: "We don't serve Iranians." At school my locker is toilet-papered. I am very confused. I thought I was an American. I am twelve years old.

(All clap.)

SAUL: 1981.

ANGEL: 1981.

LEYLA: Mexico City, Mexico.

SAUL: My father is a good provider, but he has one problem—he is an alcoholic. Many times he comes home drunk. This leads to fights with my mother. I see this over and over again. I am five years old.

(All clap.)

LEYLA: 1982.

ANGEL: 1982.

PING: 1982.

LEYLA: My brother, Khayyam, becomes a born-again Christian and changes his name from Khayyam Modir to Christian Martyr. He buys a stack of Bibles that almost reaches the ceiling. He decides to go to Iran and convert the Islamic nation. No one can convince him that this is insane. Before he leaves he gives away all of his earthly possessions. As a last ditch effort, my father sits Khayyam down and says:

ANGEL: "Khayyam, Jesus is talking through me. Do not go to Iran."

LEYLA: He doesn't go.

(All clap.)

TANIA: 1982.

ALL: 1982.

TANIA: I am applying to be a student at Boston College. I have to check one of the following boxes:

ANGEL: Caucasian,

LEYLA: Black,

PING: Hispanic,

LEYLA: Asian,

ALL: Other.

TANIA: I don't know which one to check. The administrator says to me:

ANGEL: "You are from Venezuela, so you should check Hispanic."

TANIA: But a Hispanic is someone from Spain and I'm half Lebanese, half Venezuelan, half Catholic, and half Druze from the Middle East, which is Asia Minor. I notice people talking about race and color in the United States in a way that just doesn't happen in Venezuela or Lebanon. What does it have to do with who people are?

PING: 1982.

LEYLA: 1982.

TANIA: 1982

PING: It becomes clear to me that the New York theater scene represents a white aesthetic with its roots in Europe. I don't quite fit the template or the ideology. However, the only place that embraces me completely with open arms, to this day, is La MaMa E.T.C. in New York City. Artistic director Ellen Stewart, or "MaMa," as we call her, opened her theater to the world.

ANGEL: 1983.

PING: 1983.

TANIA AND SAUL: 1983.

LEYLA: Goshen, Indiana.

ANGEL: I am seventeen years old. I get my first no-lye permanent hair relaxer. My scalp is burned so badly I have scabs for weeks, but my hair is straight.

(All clap.)

1983.

ALL: 1983.

LEYLA: Goshen High School.

ANGEL: I am one of three African Americans in a school of fifteen hundred. I never date. When I make friends with Andreas, an exchange student from Germany, he is asked:

PING: "Why are you hanging around with that nigger?"

ANGEL: I am an UNDESIRABLE ELEMENT.

(All clap.)

SAUL: 1983.

ALL: 1983.

SAUL: My mother can't take the drinking and the fighting any longer. She divorces my father and goes to the United States. My mother wants to make money to come back and start a business. She can't afford to take us with her. I am seven years old.

(All clap.)

ANGEL: 1984.

LEYLA: 1984.

PING: 1984.

TANIA: Goshen College.

ANGEL: I attend a meeting of the Black Student Union. The discussion quickly turns to the struggles with racism and discrimination the black students are facing in the community and on campus. At Town House Restaurant, a diner I have frequented for much of my life, two of my new black friends are refused service by the waitress, and some men in the next booth say:

LEYLA: "Why don't you niggers get out of town?!"

ANGEL: When the girls go to the associate dean for help, they are told:

PING: "There's no racism in Goshen."

ANGEL: I listen to their story in silence. My skin burns. I feel like an imposter. I may share their complexion, but they must see that on the inside I'm a part of the problem. I don't return to the Black Student Union.

SAUL: 1985.

TANIA AND ANGEL: 1985.

LEYLA: Chicago, Illinois.

SAUL: My mother has a hard time in the United States. She doesn't speak English, so it's hard to get a job. People look down on her because she's Mexican. Finally, she finds a job. My mother saves her money and sends it home to my grandmother to deposit for her future business in Mexico.

LEYLA: 1986.

ANGEL: 1986.

TANIA AND SAUL: 1986.

LEYLA: I'm eighteen and finally get to join the actors' union in a play called *The Immigrant*. The *Chicago Sun-Times* calls me:

PING: "an archival Ellis Island photograph come to life."

LEYLA: From then on, everywhere I perform, from Chicago to L.A., from San Francisco to Seattle, I play anyone with an accent:

TANIA: Italians,

ANGEL: Greeks,

TANIA: Russians,

SAUL: Mexicans,

PING: Chinese.

LEYLA: I usually play low-status, marginal outsiders—either funny maids or quirky orphan girls. My agent often calls saying:

ANGEL: "They need an exotic. Are you free on Tuesday?"

SAUL: 1986.

ALL: 1986.

TANIA: Mexico City, Mexico.

SAUL: My mother comes home. After working two hard years, she finds out that my grandmother has spent all the money that she had sent home. Her dream of a business in Mexico disappears. She returns to the United States.

(All clap.)

PING: 1986.

ALL: 1986.

PING: I am invited to the prestigious Toga Festival in Japan as the theater artist representing the United States. I apply to the National Endowment for the Arts for travel funds. Through the grapevine, I learn that an administrator there said:

TANIA: "Could someone with the name Ping Chong represent the United States?"

(All clap.)

1986.

LEYLA: 1986.

TANIA: 1986.

ANGEL: Japan.

PING: It is the first time that I have been in Asia since I was seventeen years old. Although Japan is not China, I still feel a deep affinity. It is the first time since I left the world of Chinatown as a young adult that I feel a sense of belonging. It is the first time as an adult that I don't stand out as the Other. In America, Asians are regarded as the model minority until there's a conflict with an Asian country. Then we're not American. Then we can't be trusted.

SAUL: 1989.

ANGEL: 1989.

LEYLA: Mexico City, Mexico.

SAUL: With no mother and an alcoholic father, I start getting into trouble. I begin selling "candy" to rich kids at a private school. The candy is actually marijuana in little plastic bags. After a while I am selling a thousand dollars worth in fifteen minutes. I am eleven years old.

(All clap.)

ANGEL: 1989.

PING: 1989.

LEYLA: 1989.

ANGEL: I move to New York City. Walking through LaGuardia Airport, hundreds of people of all colors surround me and for the first time I don't stand out as the Other. Something is lifted. I feel incredibly free.

SAUL: 1991.

TANIA: 1991.

PING: Mexico City, Mexico.

SAUL: The crime organization I work for, *La Familia*, becomes my family. For the first time, I feel a sense of belonging.
    1992.

ANGEL AND LEYLA: 1992.

SAUL: It is Christmas every Friday night at *La Familia*. One by one, we go into a special room decorated like Christmas. I think it's tacky. There are presents under the tree for us, filled with money. This is how we get paid. I graduate to selling—

ALL: Heroin!

(All clap.)

LEYLA: 1994.

ANGEL: 1994.

PING: 1994.

LEYLA: My brother, Hafez, moves his family to Tehran. I decide to visit him. People don't understand why I'm going. After the shah, Khomeini and the Iran-Iraq war, Iran is still trying to regain its equilibrium. For my relatives in Iran, it is ground zero. In 1994, most Americans don't know what it feels like to live at ground zero. Most Americans don't really want to know.

(All clap.)

SAUL: 1994.

LEYLA: 1994.

ANGEL: 1994.

TANIA: Lacandona Jungle, Mexico.

SAUL: The Indians of Mexico are:

ALL: UNDESIRABLE ELEMENTS.

SAUL: They are exploited by big businesses in collusion with the government.

PING: They are threatened with violence.

TANIA: They are not allowed to own land, even though they are the true guardians of the land.

LEYLA: They are deprived of medical, educational and social services.

ANGEL: They are treated as the lowest level of Mexican society.

SAUL: *Los Zapatistas*, an indigenous people's movement, grows. With some of the drug money I earn, I buy clothes, shoes, medicine and other supplies for them. I am sixteen years old.

(All clap.)

1994.

ALL: 1994.

LEYLA: Mexico City. New Year's Eve.

SAUL: *Los Zapatistas* holds a national news conference on television to fight for the rights of the people. They want the world to know that they are not terrorists.

(All clap.)

PING: 1995.

ANGEL: 1995.

TANIA: 1995.

LEYLA: Why is Hong Kong being returned to China?

ANGEL: Why don't they just let the British keep it?

PING: I realize how little Americans know about the cause and effects of history in relationship to China—why it is hard for the Chinese to trust the West. I decide to create a production entitled *Chinoiserie*, which includes

TANIA: the racially motivated murder of Vincent Chin in Detroit,

LEYLA: the blatant violence perpetuated against the Chinese-American pioneers,

ANGEL: and the Opium Wars—when China fought against the British, who were illegally importing opium into the country.

LEYLA: China lost the war. As a result, Hong Kong was ceded to the British for ninety-nine years.

PING: Of *Chinoiserie*, the *Village Voice* critic says:

ANGEL: "Ping Chong is too angry."

PING: The *New York Times* critic says:

TANIA: "Ping Chong is not angry enough."

PING: The *Arts Asia* critic, who is Chinese, says:

LEYLA: "Ping Chong got it right."

(All clap.)

SAUL: 1995.

PING: 1995.

ANGEL: Mexico City, Mexico.

SAUL: I break the first rule of drug dealing, which is—

ALL: NEVER USE DRUGS!

SAUL: I try marijuana first, then cocaine, and then angel dust.

SAUL: 1995.

ALL: 1995.

SAUL: A friend from *La Familia* says:

ANGEL: "Saul, come with us. We're going to show you the way we do things."

SAUL: We are driving down a street. We pass a store with a couple of guys playing dominoes outside. Before I know it, the guy sitting next to me pulls out a machine gun and the guy in front pulls out a pistol. When I look back, people are screaming. I'm in shock.

ANGEL: "Okay, now you're one of us. We're going to give you a gun."

SAUL: My friend stops him.

TANIA: "No, no, wait a minute, let me talk to him."

SAUL: Later he says:

TANIA: "Crime pays, but you don't live long enough to enjoy it. Right now you can get out, but once you cross the line, there's no turning back. You better make a choice."

SAUL: 1995.

ALL: 1995.

TANIA: Mexico City, Mexico.

SAUL: My drug abuse is making me violent. To scare a teacher in class, I grab a chair and throw it out of a window. My father says:

PING: "Saul, I'm sending you to live with your mother in the United States."

(All clap.)

SAUL: 1997.

ALL: 1997.

ANGEL: Atlanta, Georgia.

TANIA: "Saul, it's time to get up."

SAUL: My mom calls my name again:

TANIA: "Saul, get up. You have to go . . ."

SAUL: When she calls my name a third time:

TANIA: "Saul Alejandro Avina, wake up!"

SAUL: Whoa! When my mom says my full name, she means business. We get into the car and she drives me straight to—

ALL: School!

SAUL: She had been planning this all along. She says:

TANIA: "Your dad and uncles are talking about a lot of bad things that you've been doing. Now, you have a chance at a new life."

(All clap.)

ANGEL: 1998.

ALL: 1998.

ANGEL: I am accepted into the MFA program in theater management at Yale School of Drama. Almost overnight, I go from the multicultural environment I so enjoyed in New York to the white, Eurocentric regional theater environment of the drama school. I realize that, as the sole person of color in my class of seven theater managers, I represent a quota. In class, when the discussion turns to subjects like diversity, multiculturalism, racism, race *anything*, I'm on the spot:

PING: "Angel, don't you have anything to say?"

TANIA: "Angel, what do you think?"

LEYLA: "Angel, how does this make *you* feel?"

ANGEL: I feel pissed off. I'm here to learn, not to teach!

(*All clap.*)

TANIA: 1998.

ALL: 1998.

ANGEL: Venezuela.

TANIA: The United States and Iraq, Iraq and the United States. On cable television we pick a Lebanese news program about the continuing Gulf War. We also watch the news on CNN, but the reporting is totally different. On CNN, we learn that the United States is careful not to hit civilian targets. On the Lebanese news program, we learn that civilian targets are the first to get hit.

ALL: Who's telling the truth?

SAUL: 1998.

ALL: 1998.

SAUL: My mom says:

TANIA: "Okay, don't talk to the blacks because they're bad. Talk to the white people, they will help you."

SAUL: So, I start hanging out with the white kids. They ask me:

ANGEL: "How many brothers and sisters do you have, wetback?"

SAUL: "Only three."

PING: "I thought you people lived twenty in an apartment."

SAUL: "Oh, no, only my mother and me."

LEYLA: "Why don't you go back to Mexico?"

SAUL: "Mexico, okay, maybe I'll go back next year." I don't realize they're being racist. Finally I start to make friends with some African Americans, too. I take the color tape off my eyes. I don't want to be with just one group of people. It would only make my world smaller.

(*All clap ten times. Blackout.*
    Beat.
    Quiet, plaintive flute music begins to play in the background.
    Lights up. One by one, each performer recites a poem in his/her native language. These poems are not translated, but create a

medley of different languages and sounds. The flute music plays throughout. After the concluding poem, Leyla speaks:)

LEYLA: You can choose anything in the world you want, my child, but you can never choose your heritage.

(All clap ten times.)

TANIA *(In Arabic):* إذا بتريدوا أقفوا.

(All rise. They change seats, walking single file around the outer perimeter of the semi-circle as the Norwegian incantation is repeated.)

إذا بتريدوا أقعدوا.

(All sit and open their scripts.)

SAUL: 1999.

ALL: 1999.

SAUL: I volunteer for a Domestic Violence Prevention Program with Georgia State, to work with kids from troubled families. On the first day, the facilitator says:

PING: "Saul, first we start with sharing."

SAUL: The children share their stories and experiences as survivors of physical and emotional abuse. For the first time, I see myself as a child of abuse. I didn't know there was a name for it. I share my story with the kids. I tell them about my father's alcohol abuse, how he never cared for me emotionally. An eight-year-old kid reaches over and comforts me. I feel a great release.

(All clap.)

PING: 2000.

ALL: 2000.

PING: I am working on the fifteenth production of *Undesirable Elements*, for Charleston, South Carolina. This particular production emphasizes the untold history of racism and slavery in Charleston. Until 1999, there wasn't a single public monument for the suffering of African Americans. And when one is finally created, it is a small plaque near a parking lot. If you blink, you might miss it. While working on *Undesirable Elements*, I have the first of many experiences of what it means to be black in

Charleston today. I am walking down a street with my African-American lighting designer, Darren McCroom. A white College of Charleston student is walking toward us.

TANIA: One,

LEYLA: two,

ANGEL: three seconds pass.

PING: He spits on the ground.

TANIA: Seconds later Darren says:

ANGEL: "You know what that means?"

PING: "No, I don't."

ANGEL: "It means nigger."

(All clap.)

SAUL: 2000.

ALL: 2000.

LEYLA: Atlanta, Georgia.

SAUL: I am shopping at Lenox Mall.

TANIA: Within minutes, Saul is aware that he is not shopping alone.

SAUL: One of the white salespeople is following me.

PING: Now, when Saul enters a store, he says:

SAUL: "Yeah, I'm Mexican. Don't worry. I'm not going to steal anything. I have money."

(All clap.)

TANIA: 2000.

ALL: 2000.

LEYLA: Beirut, Lebanon.

TANIA: I return to Lebanon for the first time in nine years. There are still no streetlights. There are still bombed-out buildings, but there is still hope. I lost a lot of neighbors, friends and family—Muslim, Christian and Druze—to the war. I had to grow up really fast. To this day, I finish all the food on my plate as if the war was still going on. I realize I have a habit of living right here, right now, as if there might be no tomorrow.

(All clap.)

SAUL: 2001.

ALL: 2001.

SAUL: I have a new life now. I work as a counselor helping kids overcome violence in their lives. I don't look like a teacher or a therapist, so kids feel like they can talk to me.

(All clap.)

ANGEL: 2001.
ALL: 2001.
TANIA: September 11, 2001.
PING: New York City.
ANGEL: My phone is ringing and ringing and ringing. Finally, I get out of bed and check my messages. By the time I turn on the television, the first World Trade Center tower is already down. A few short minutes later, I watch the second tower fall. I am three miles from Ground Zero.

(All clap.)

LEYLA: 2001.
ALL: 2001.
LEYLA: The months following 9/11 are filled with despairing events. Students drop out of my sister-in-law's class because her name is Yeganeh Modirzadeh and she wears a *hejab*. My friend, Shoaleh's brother, is pulled off of an Amtrak train and interrogated by the FBI for talking on his cell phone in Farsi. My uncles change their names from Mohammed to Steve and Mike. My best friend's ten-year-old son asks me where my family is from. I say my father is Iranian. He points his toy gun at me and says:
PING: "Ooh, those are bad people."

(All clap.)

TANIA: 2001.
ALL: 2001.
PING: October 25, 2001.
TANIA: My father is killed in an accident. I fly to Lebanon. On the plane, I sit next to a Muslim woman. I can't stop crying. She says:
ANGEL: "Whatever it is, it's not worth so many tears."
TANIA: I tell her that my father and uncle have been killed in a car accident. She cries with me and puts my head to rest on her lap, caressing my hair, while singing from the Koran. I fall asleep.

(All clap.)

2001.

ALL: 2001.

PING: Beirut, Lebanon.

TANIA: I hear many stories about my father's life. People come to mourn from eight o'clock in the morning until eleven at night. The funeral is beautiful—the *sheikhas* chanting, the women telling poems. When I return to New York, I discover that I am four months pregnant. I wasn't aware; I hadn't felt a thing. My husband and I name our daughter Naima, which means "soft." In ancient Arabic it means "Allah's miracle."

(All clap.)

SAUL: 2003.

ALL: 2003.

SAUL: I am still working as a counselor at the domestic violence program, but things are changing. The government is cutting funding for social programs. We have to start charging for services that were free.

(All clap.)

TANIA: 2003.

ALL: 2003.

SAUL: New York City.

TANIA: Discrimination against Muslims, and people who look like Muslims, continues. I don't want my daughter, Naima, to grow up in a place that mocks her culture, that treats her as the enemy. I don't want her to deny her heritage. At the same time, my visa expires and I will have to pay three thousand five hundred dollars every year to stay. The INS discriminates against those of us who aren't rich. My husband Thomas, who is English, and I decide to leave the U.S. But where should we go?

(All clap.)

SAUL: 2004.

ALL: 2004.

ANGEL: Mexico City.

SAUL: I go back to Mexico to visit my family. All the friends that I used to have no longer exist. They are dead, in jail or living on the streets. It is like there is no trace of my past. I feel like everything has changed, but I am the one who has changed. When my family looks at me they see

TANIA: crazy hair,

PING: tattoos—

ANGEL: *eighteen* tattoos!

SAUL: I'm trying to tell a story with my body. Every tattoo is symbolic of my life, of where I've been and where I am going. But they just see a criminal-looking guy with crazy ideas. My dad accuses my mother of turning me into a *pordiosero*—

ALL: A bum!

(All clap.)

TANIA: 2006.

ALL: 2006.

PING: Lebanon.

TANIA: Israel bombs Lebanon. I watch the news from London and telephone my family in Beirut every day to see if they are alive. As soon as the blockade is lifted, I fly to Lebanon with my two daughters. There is destruction everywhere I look.

(All clap.)

2006.

ALL: 2006.

SAUL: Lebanon.

TANIA: We are driving through the destroyed parts of South Beirut when my four-year-old daughter Naima asks me:

LEYLA: "Why are all these houses broken?"

TANIA: I say:

ANGEL: "Sometimes people get upset with each other and break each other's houses. Those who hurt and break people's houses are bad people."

LEYLA: "No, Mummy, that's not possible. All the people are beautiful!"

(All clap.)

ANGEL: 2006.

ALL: 2006.

ANGEL: I am back in New York City, the city of my birth, the city that is now home. I am no longer an outsider in my own community, for New York is the ultimate community of outsiders. I've learned to be grateful for the sometimes painful awareness that comes from being an Other, because with this awareness comes freedom—freedom to view the world from a place of empathy. Goshen, Indiana, has changed, too. An influx of immigrants from Ecuador, Colombia, Mexico, has changed the face of that community forever. Goshen High School, where I once stood out as one of three African Americans, is almost forty percent Latino. Now, when I return to Goshen, people speak Spanish to me on the street and assume I know what they are saying.

(All clap.)

SAUL: 2006.

ALL: 2006.

SAUL: I am now a United States citizen, so I can work for social change here. But I am still proud to call myself Mexican. At the end of the day, I'm not Hispanic, Latino or "illegal alien." I am and always will be Mexican. But if you ask me where my home is, it is not Mexico, and it is not the U.S. Home is wherever I stand.

(All clap.)

LEYLA: 2006.

ALL: 2006.

LEYLA: When I think of my cultural identity, I scan my ancestors from Jew to Muslim to Catholic, from Irish, South African, Russian, Iranian . . . and I come up with human being. If I'm hurt, it's because I'm human. If I'm outraged, it's because I'm human. And if I'm hopeful, which I am, it isn't because of nationalism, but because I'm human. I live in America and identify as an American, but I prefer a world identity where I can let go of all borders, past and present, and stop asking where anyone is from, because it will be obvious that we are all from the same place.

(All clap.)

TANIA: 2006.

ALL: 2006.

TANIA: I have a recurring dream. I am walking into my family home in Beirut. I am standing alone in the foyer that has no windows. When I try to go into the rest of the apartment, I cannot. Maybe, one day, I will be able to.

(All clap.)

PING: 2006.
ALL: 2006.
PING: Time passes. I am now fifty-eight years old. I look in the mirror and I see my father's face filling into mine. We are finally connected. I live roughly ten city blocks away from Chinatown, in the former enemy territory of Little Italy. When I'm not on tour, I am in Chinatown shopping for fresh produce in the marketplace, along with all the thrifty Chinese housewives. If you walk on Elizabeth Street, you can see me, a graying middle-aged Chinese man, coming back from Chinatown with the tell-tale red plastic bags filled with the essence of his being. If he's not on Elizabeth Street, then he may be taking off for Denmark, Italy, Japan, El Salvador—because he's a citizen of the world and, beyond all labels, a human being.

(All clap ten times. An uplifting choral song begins to play softly in the background. It continues through the finale.)

LEYLA: My name is Leyla Modirzadeh. I was born on June 30, 1967, at 5:30 P.M., in Durham, North Carolina. The delivering doctor told my mother, "Hurry up! I want to go home and have dinner." It was the summer of love.
　　Saul?

(She closes her script and stands.)

SAUL: My name is Saul Alejandro Avina. I was born September 18, 1978, in Mexico City, Mexico, during the week we celebrate Independence Day. I am the youngest of three siblings.
　　Tania?

(He closes his script and stands.)

TANIA: My name is Tania Salmen. I was born to a Druze father and a Christian mother, on November 2, 1963, in Maturin, Vene-

zuela, *en El Dia De Los Muertos*, on the Day of the Dead. A horse named Tania won a race that day. It was the rainy season.
　Ping?

(She closes her script and stands.)

PING: My name is Ping Chong. I was born in Toronto, Canada, on October 2, 1946. I share a birthday with Groucho Marx and Mahatma Gandhi. I was named Gordon by the hospital doctor, but my mother couldn't pronounce it, so I became John Ping Chong. It was autumn.
　Angel?

(He closes his script and stands.)

ANGEL: My name is Angela Beth Gardner. I was born on January 20, 1966, in New York City, USA. When the social worker placed me in my parents' arms for the first time, they said, "She's such a little angel." It must have been winter.

(She closes her script and stands.
Music up. The performers face the audience and repeat their gestures from the beginning of the performance, raising, crossing and lowering their arms slowly and gracefully in unison, as the lights fade to black.)

END

Inside/Out . . . voices from the disability community

Washington, D.C. / 2008

Written and directed by Ping Chong and Sara Zatz

IN COLLABORATION WITH:

Josh Hecht

Monique Holt*

Christopher Imbrosciano

Vivian Cary Jenkins

Matthew S. Joffe

Zazel Chavah O'Garra

Blair Wing

*The voice actress for Monique Holt was Mindy Pearl Pfeffer

After the creation of *Children of War* in 2002, the *Undesirable Elements* series continued to expand thematically, including projects that specifically focused on Asian-American identity and Native American identity. In 2006, I created *Undesirable Elements/ Albuquerque*, a piece that featured several performers with disabilities, although it wasn't the entire focus of the piece. I had been interested in working with people with disabilities and, specifically, with the Deaf community, ever since I worked with the National Theater of the Deaf in the late 1990s. I recognized disability as a significant area of experience that is rarely acknowledged or discussed in conversations about civil society and social justice, and even more rarely explored in theatrical settings. I felt there was even more to be discussed, and Ping Chong + Company approached VSA, an international arts organization dedicated to promoting accessibility and understanding through the arts. VSA then commissioned a new *Undesirable Elements* entirely dedicated to the experiences of people with disabilities. The result was *Inside/Out . . . voices from the disability community*. I found this project to be particularly poignant as disability impacts all segments of our society, regardless of cultural background, and we have to recognize that most of us will have a disability at some point in our lifetime, or be in a position to care for a loved one with a disability, even if it is just by reaching old age.

—*Ping Chong*

PRODUCTION HISTORY

Inside/Out . . . voices from the disability community premiered at the John F. Kennedy Center for the Performing Arts in Washington, D.C., on June 27, 2008. It was conceived by Ping Chong. It was directed by Ping Chong and Sara Zatz. It was written by Ping Chong and Sara Zatz, in collaboration with the performers. The lighting designer/technical director was Brant Thomas Murray and the stage manager was Courtney Golden. The company interpreter was Timothy Chamberlain. The performers were Josh Hecht, Monique Holt, Christopher Imbrosicano, Vivian Cary Jenkins, Matthew S. Joffe, Zazel Chavah O'Garra and Blair Wing. Mindy Pearl Pfeffer was the voice actress for Monique Holt.

Inside/Out was commissioned, funded and produced by VSA. The Executive Producer was Elena Widder and the Associate Producer was Elizabeth McCloskey Miller. Rehearsals were supported, in part, by a space grant from LaGuardia Performing Arts Center, in Long Island City, New York, where *Inside/Out* was presented for a public work-in-progress reading. Additional support for the *Undesirable Elements* series came from the National Endowment for the Arts, New York State Council on the Arts, New York City Department of Cultural Affairs, The Nathan Cummings Foundation and MetLife Foundation.

Eight music stands and seven chairs stand upstage, arranged in a curve, around a white semicircle. Each music stand holds a copy of the script, which the performers read from throughout the performance. None of the performers ever leaves the stage.

Lights slowly come up. A haunting Norwegian incantation plays. One at a time, the performers approach their music stand. The first performer to enter uses a wheelchair and takes her place at the music stand without a chair in front of it. When all have reached their music stands, the incantation fades and lights come up.

BLAIR: Let's get started! Please sit.

(*All sit.*)

My name is Elizabeth Blair Wing. I was born on May 21, 1974, in Poughkeepsie, New York. It was spring.
Josh?
JOSH: My name is Joshua Eric Hecht. I was born on June 5, 1978, at 3:45 P.M. in New York City. It was spring.
Mindy?
MINDY: My name is Mindy Pearl Pfeffer and I am the voice actress for Monique Holt.
Vivian?

VIVIAN: My name is Vivian Cary Jenkins. I was born in Brooklyn, New York, in Beth-El Hospital on May 31, 1943, at 7:45 P.M. It was spring.
Zazel?

ZAZEL: My name is Zazel Chavah O'Garra. I was born on January 5, 1963, in Jamaica, Queens. It was winter.
Monique?

(Monique's lines are in American Sign Language [ASL], voiced simultaneously by Mindy Pfeffer.)

MONIQUE: My name is Monique Bok Holt. The details of my birth are unknown.
Chris?

CHRISTOPHER: My name is Christopher Imbrosciano. I was born on July 27, 1984, in Edison, New Jersey. It was summer.
Matthew?

MATTHEW: My name is Matthew Seth Joffe. I was born on June 15, 1953, in New York City. It was spring.

(All clap ten times.)

CHRISTOPHER: What do people think?
ZAZEL: What do people think?
JOSH: What do people think?
MONIQUE: What do people think?
BLAIR: What do people think of when they hear the word . . .
VIVIAN: "Disability"?
ZAZEL: Cripple.
CHRISTOPHER: Handicapped.
MATTHEW: Lame.
BLAIR: Retard.
MONIQUE: Moron.
CHRISTOPHER: Gimp.
MATTHEW: Freak.
JOSH: Weak.
ZAZEL: Challenged.
VIVIAN: Dependent.
CHRISTOPHER: Special.
MATTHEW: Short-bus!
BLAIR: Human being.

(All clap.)

JOSH: Trepanation.

ALL: Trepanation:

VIVIAN: the boring of a hole through the skull. As practiced by ancient Andean peoples, it was a form of advanced brain surgery.

JOSH: Trepanation had a survival rate that rivals brain surgery under today's modern medicine.

(All clap.)

BLAIR: Multiple sclerosis.

ALL: Multiple sclerosis:

CHRISTOPHER: a mysterious chronic disease of the central nervous system that is very difficult to diagnose. Three of the classic symptoms are:

ALL: One:

ZAZEL: dysarthria—

CHRISTOPHER: problems with speech.

ALL: Two:

ZAZEL: ataxia—

BLAIR: problems with coordination.

ALL: Three:

JOSH: tremors.

(All clap.)

ALL *(Speaking and then signing in American Sign Language)*: Ball! Strike! Safe! Yer Out!

(All clap.)

BLAIR: In the late nineteenth century, baseball became America's pastime. William Ellsworth "Dummy" Hoy was the first deaf player in the major leagues and one of the best players of his era.

MATTHEW: One day he asked an umpire to use hand signals when announcing a call and changed baseball forever.

VIVIAN: The signals the umpires developed, some incorporated from American Sign Language, are now used all over the world.

(All clap.)

JOSH: Moebius.

ALL: Moebius.

MONIQUE: Syndrome.

ALL: Syndrome.

BLAIR: Moebius syndrome.

ALL: Moebius syndrome.

CHRISTOPHER: Moebius syndrome is a rare neurological disorder that is present at birth. Those with the condition are unable to smile, frown, suck, grimace, blink or move their lips. Symptoms may include:

ZAZEL: lack of facial expression,

MONIQUE: drooling,

ZAZEL: hand and foot deformities,

MONIQUE: eye sensitivity,

ZAZEL: motor delays.

MATTHEW: I am one of one thousand people in the United States born with Moebius syndrome.

(All clap.)

MONIQUE: R-E-T-I-N-A.

ALL: R-E-T-I-N-A.

CHRISTOPHER: What is the retina?

BLAIR: The retina is the layer of tissue that lines the back of the eye. It functions much as film does in a camera, receiving images via the optic nerve to the brain.

JOSH: If the film in a camera is defective, the image cannot be developed. This is also true with the camera known as:

CHRISTOPHER: the human eye.

(All clap.)

VIVIAN: William Little, a nineteenth-century English surgeon, was the first to describe a strange disorder in children causing

MATTHEW: involuntary and spastic movement of the limbs,

VIVIAN: muscle tone that is either too stiff or too floppy,

MATTHEW: seizures.

VIVIAN: This condition was known as Little's disease.

MATTHEW: The scientific name today is spastic diplegia.

VIVIAN: It is one of a family of disorders known under the umbrella term "cerebral palsy."

CHRISTOPHER: I have cerebral palsy.

(All clap.)

ZAZEL: The earliest known image of a wheelchair dates back to a carving on a sarcophagus from sixth-century China.

CHRISTOPHER: Over a thousand years later, the image of the wheelchair will become the internationally recognized symbol for:

ALL *(Speaking and signing in ASL)*: ACCESS!

(All clap ten times. Blackout.
  Beat.
  Lights up.)

BLAIR: 1927.

ALL: 1927.

JOSH: The United States Supreme Court declares:

BLAIR: "The forced sterilization of people with disabilities is not a violation of their constitutional rights."

JOSH: Over the next fifty years more than sixty thousand people will be sterilized without their consent. They are considered

ALL *(Speaking and signing in ASL)*: UNDESIRABLE ELEMENTS.

VIVIAN: 1933.

ALL: 1933.

MATTHEW: President Franklin Delano Roosevelt is sworn in as the thirty-second President of the United States. He walks with braces or uses a wheelchair—a result of polio he contracted in 1921—but he is never photographed in a wheelchair in public. Most Americans are unaware that their president has a disability:

BLAIR: It would be seen as a sign of weakness in a great leader.

ZAZEL: 1947.

ALL: 1947.

JOSH: Pennsylvania.

MONIQUE: A young girl named Catherine attends Mount Airy School for the Deaf. She learns to speak and read lips. The students have to sit on their hands so they can't sign. If they sign, they are punished. She doesn't know it yet, but she will become my adoptive mother.

(All clap.)

CHRISTOPHER: 1951.

ALL: 1951.

BLAIR: New York City.

VIVIAN: I am eight years old, a Jewish Brooklynite taking ballet classes in Manhattan. I love ballet! On Saturdays my father picks me up after class and we explore the city. We eat forbidden non-kosher foods with pork and we mix meat and milk:

MATTHEW: hamburgers with milkshakes,

CHRISTOPHER: bacon, lettuce and tomato sandwiches,

JOSH: Chinese food.

VIVIAN: My mother never joins us. She would disapprove.

BLAIR: 1954.

ALL: 1954.

MATTHEW: I am one year old. My mouth is open and doesn't close. My head tilts forward or to the side. I can't hold it up. Eating is difficult. My mother takes me to a doctor. He has no idea what my problem is. He says:

JOSH: "Matthew should be institutionalized. You shouldn't waste any time on him. He'll be dead in a year."

MONIQUE: 1958.

ALL: 1958.

MATTHEW: During an office visit, several doctors' residents come in to observe me. They all crowd around me to get a good look, like I am an animal in the zoo. Do they ever consider how their staring makes me feel? I am five years old.

JOSH: 1961.

ALL: 1961.

MATTHEW: I have the first of ten surgeries related to Moebius syndrome. My parents refuse to treat me like a child with a disability. They take me to movies, the theater, to restaurants, so that I am not sheltered from the world. They watch my back and defend me. They never give up on me.

(All clap two times.)

BLAIR: 1963.

ALL: 1963.

VIVIAN: I never doubted that I would be a dancer, but I don't have the fire in the belly that it takes to succeed in dance. Opportunities are few, salaries are low, and I have to work to help support my family. What should I do instead?

JOSH: 1966.

ALL: 1966.

CHRISTOPHER: Mattlin Junior High School.

MATTHEW: I am tormented and alienated by the other children. Steven, one of my only friends, is teased for hanging out with me. One day three boys jump Steven. He is sent to the assistant principal's office for fighting.

ALL: One, two, three, four,

BLAIR: five minutes pass.

MATTHEW: Steven tells me:

CHRISTOPHER: "I'm going to be suspended."

MATTHEW: I tell the assistant principal:

JOSH: "I don't like fighting, but it's not fair for Steven to be punished just because he chooses me as a friend."

MATTHEW: Steven is not suspended after all. From this experience I learn to stand up for myself and others. I am thirteen years old.

(All clap two times.)

CHRISTOPHER: 1967.

ALL: 1967.

MONIQUE: New York City.

ZAZEL: Because my parents are from the West Indies, I grow up with an accent. At school, I am teased because of my accent, my high cheekbones, large lips, nappy hair and colorful clothes. I feel like an outsider.

ALL: 1967.

MATTHEW: Honduras.

ZAZEL: Barrio Medina.

VIVIAN: I join the Peace Corps and am sent to Honduras. When we ask the local people what they want, they say:

CHRISTOPHER: "We want to build a park for the children."

VIVIAN: While there are many needs in this poor community, this is the one that's closest to their hearts. We help them plan and raise money for the park. I become aware I have a talent for:

MONIQUE: organizing,

JOSH: directing,

MONIQUE: managing.

(All clap ten times.)

BLAIR: Vivian?

VIVIAN: Yes, Blair?

BLAIR: What do *you* think of when you hear the word "disability"?

VIVIAN: Dependence, courage, fear, pity, strength, isolation, growth, respect, admiration, exhaustion, limitation, reinvention.

(All clap two times.)

ALL: 1968.

BLAIR: New York City.

JOSH: Elena Sue Sadock is a feisty, independent young woman. She wants to be a doctor. She is accepted to medical school but her father says:

MATTHEW: "Women shouldn't work. They should stay home and raise children. If you must work, become a nurse or teacher."

CHRISTOPHER: 1969.

ALL: 1969.

MONIQUE: Henry and Catherine Holt adopt a deaf Korean girl named Yoon Bok Hyun. When the chaperone hands me over to Henry at the airport, I am so scared I pee on him. I am three years old.

JOSH: 1969.

ALL: 1969.

CHRISTOPHER: To make sure Zazel behaves, her mom says:

BLAIR: "Zazel, what's done in darkness will come to light."

CHRISTOPHER: She also says:

BLAIR: "Zazel, don't listen to what other people say about you. Always hold your head up high."

ZAZEL: My mother works as a nurse's aide at Bird S. Coler Hospital from midnight till seven A.M. Before she leaves, she prepares a delicious West Indian dinner for my father, my sister and me:

MONIQUE: salt fish with dumplings,

BLAIR: boiled kingfish with corn fungi,

MONIQUE: washed down with ginger beer or sorrel juice.

ZAZEL: I never learn to make dumplings because I love them too much. If I make them, I will eat them all!

CHRISTOPHER: 1970.

ALL: 1970.

JOSH: Jay Hecht, a teacher, meets Elena Sue Sadock, now also a teacher. He is a straight arrow with his feet on the ground; she is bright, vivacious and a little wild. Opposites attract: Jay and Elena, Elena and Jay. If they had not met that day, I would not be here now. They will become my parents.

(All clap.)

BLAIR: 1971.

ALL: 1971.

MATTHEW: It's summer. I go with my mother and sister to the swimming pool to get our season passes. My mother asks me to go inside and pick them up. When I ask for the passes, the woman at the ticket window, who has watched me grow up at the pool, says repeatedly:

MONIQUE: "Where's your mother?"

ZAZEL: "Where's your mother?"

BLAIR: "Where's your mother?"

MATTHEW: She refuses to give me the passes. I say:

CHRISTOPHER: "Lady, I have a double major and speak two languages. What is your problem?"

MATTHEW: She gives me the passes. Clearly, looks can be deceiving.

(All clap two times.)

VIVIAN: 1971.

ALL: 1971.

MONIQUE: I am watching *Swan Lake* on TV; I fall in love with dance. I say to my father:

ZAZEL: "That is what I want to do. I want to dance."

MONIQUE: My father says:

MATTHEW: "You can't dance because you can't hear the music."

MONIQUE: I never take a formal dance class, but it doesn't stop me from dancing.

JOSH: 1972.

ALL: 1972.

ZAZEL: Every Saturday my mother takes me from Queens to Harlem to the Ruth Williams Dance Studio. I take tap and ballet. I like tap, but I *love* ballet!

BLAIR: 1972.

ALL: 1972.

JOSH: Elena is a life force. She dazzles Jay. She introduces him to progressive rock music and liberal politics. She even introduces him to iced coffee. She buys him a blue velvet suit to wear to the opera. Her family doesn't know how to contain her erratic enthusiasm. What are they going to do with her?

CHRISTOPHER: 1972.

ALL: 1972.

JOSH: Berkeley, California.

VIVIAN: Times are changing: Neil Armstrong has landed on the moon, the Civil Rights Movement and the Women's Movement are underway.

BLAIR: Berkeley is a hot bed of civil rights protests. People with disabilities are fighting for their civil rights, too. Ed Roberts and a group known as the Rolling Quads establish the Independent Living Movement. At the same time, actions by other disability activists spring up nationwide.

(*All clap two times.*)

ZAZEL: 1972.

ALL: 1972.

JOSH: *Real* men excel at sports.

MATTHEW: I can't excel at sports.

JOSH: *Real* men are handy.

MATTHEW: I can't hammer a nail into a wall.

JOSH: *Real* men have a different girlfriend every week.

MATTHEW: I don't have any girlfriends.

JOSH: *Real* men don't talk about their feelings.

MATTHEW: I talk about my feelings. All through high school and college I torment myself with the following question:

JOSH: "Are you a *real* man?"

(*All clap.*)

ZAZEL: 1972.

ALL: 1972.

MONIQUE: My mother tries to expose my brother and me to Asian culture, but there isn't really any around, except for the local Chinese restaurant. My mom's friend, Kim, invites us to socialize with other Koreans at her church. Unfortunately, I don't know Korean and they don't know ASL. Everyone means well, but it just doesn't work.

ZAZEL: 1972.

ALL: 1972.

MONIQUE: We attend a public school that has a deaf program. We are the only Asian students at our school. The hearing kids make fun of us. They make their eyes slanty and do karate moves when we walk by. I feel like an outsider.

CHRISTOPHER: 1972.

ALL: 1972.

VIVIAN: Congress passes the Rehabilitation Act—the first legislation to protect people with disabilities against discrimination—but President Richard Nixon vetoes the act.

MATTHEW: Disability activists take action across the country. In New York, Pride and Disabled in Action shut down Madison Avenue and take over Nixon's headquarters the day before the election.

BLAIR: 1973.

ALL: 1973.

CHRISTOPHER: Congress overrides Nixon's veto and the Rehabilitation Act becomes law. It is only the beginning.

ALL: Change comes slowly.

(All clap.)

BLAIR: 1974.

ALL: 1974.

JOSH: Elena and Jay are in love. They marry at the St. Regis Hotel and walk into the future—their backs to the past, arm in arm, laughing.

CHRISTOPHER: How long can this happiness last?

ZAZEL: One,

MONIQUE: two,

ZAZEL: three months pass.

JOSH: Elena is walking down the street.

MONIQUE: What can possibly go wrong?

JOSH: Suddenly her right leg starts to drag.

ZAZEL: What can possibly happen next?

JOSH: She loses her balance.

MONIQUE: One,

ZAZEL: two,

MONIQUE: three,

ZAZEL: four days pass.

JOSH: It disappears. Vanishes. Gone.

(All clap.)

BLAIR: 1976.

ALL: 1976.

CHRISTOPHER: Lancaster, Pennsylvania.

MONIQUE: Hearing educators decide it is better to teach deaf children using a system called Signed Exact English, known as SEE. It bastardizes American Sign Language into English word order. Imagine putting English into Japanese grammar—it doesn't make sense! These educators don't recognize ASL is a language with its own grammar. If I use ASL at school, I get in trouble. If I use SEE at home, I get in trouble. I am very confused.

JOSH: 1977.

ALL: 1977.

VIVIAN: I am thirty-five years old and raising a family, but I want more. I want to do something that makes a difference in the world. I'm surprised that I want to be a boss, to have power. I decide to go to graduate school to become a health care administrator.

MATTHEW: 1977.

ALL: 1977.

BLAIR: "Zazel, your hips are too big!"

VIVIAN: "You've got a West Indian Body!"

MONIQUE: "You need to lose weight! You're too fat!"

ZAZEL: I attend the High School of the Performing Arts. It's *brutal*. You are always being humiliated and criticized in front of everybody. Teachers make me crazy, but I don't let them stop me, I don't let *anything* stop me, so I eat only three oatmeal cookies and a Diet Coke a day. When I go from one hundred and thirty pounds to one hundred and fifteen, my instructor says:

BLAIR: "Zazel, you look lovely!"

(All clap ten times.)

CHRISTOPHER: Matthew?

MATTHEW: Yes, Chris?

CHRISTOPHER: What do *you* think of when you hear the word "disability"?

MATTHEW: It stresses the lack of ability, which in turn overshadows a person's abilities. Why must we categorize people in the first place, let alone focus on their deficits? Often a disability is grounds for, at the very least, misunderstanding, and, at its worst, discrimination, prejudice and alienation.

(All clap two times.)

MONIQUE: Zazel?

ZAZEL: Yes, Monique?

MONIQUE: What do *you* think of when you hear the word "disability"?

ZAZEL: P-O-S-S-I-B-I-L-I-T-Y. Possibility.

(All clap two times.)

ALL: 1978.

MONIQUE: In middle school, I don't have an interpreter, so I have to sit in the front of all my classes and lip-read. When I have questions, I have to write them down for the teacher. I am eager to learn, but it's hard. I beg my parents to send me to a deaf school.

JOSH: 1978.

ALL: 1978.

ZAZEL: I get a scholarship to Dance Theatre of Harlem. George Balanchine's wife, Tanaquil Le Clercq, is the taskmaster. She uses a wheelchair, but nobody ever thinks of her as disabled. She rolls her chair under your leg to see if you can keep it extended indefinitely, which, by the way, is excruciating.

VIVIAN: 1978.

ALL: 1978.

CHRISTOPHER: New York City.

JOSH: International Center for the Disabled.

MATTHEW: I am hired as the very first full-time reading specialist in the metropolitan area to work with people who have lost the ability to speak, read or write.

(All clap two times.)

MONIQUE: 1979.

ALL: 1979.

ZAZEL: How long can happiness last?

JOSH: The loss of balance comes back to Elena, my mother. The dragging foot comes back. She is diagnosed with multiple sclerosis. She withdraws from teaching and later will withdraw from life as well.

BLAIR: 1980.

ALL: 1980.

JOSH: Washington, D.C.

MONIQUE: I finally convince my parents to send me to Model Secondary School for the Deaf. At MSSD, all the students and teachers sign. There is no need for interpreters. We have our own language. The students are from all over the country and all over the world: black, white, Asian, city kids, rural kids. For the first time, I do not feel like an outsider. I begin to find my own identity.

(All clap two times.)

CHRISTOPHER: 1980.

ALL: 1980.

MATTHEW: I see a therapist. She helps me accept myself by challenging society's narrow view of what a "real" man should be. She helps me understand that relationships are not only about sex. She helps me access the anger and rage I have built up over a lifetime of internalized self-hatred.

ZAZEL: 1980.

ALL: 1980.

JOSH: It's my second birthday. My mother is holding me in her lap. She is whispering in my ear. My mother is struggling to give out slices of cake. Her hands are trembling. This is all caught on videotape.

MONIQUE: 1980.

ALL: 1980.

CHRISTOPHER: One of the most popular shows on TV is *The Facts of Life*, about four girls at a boarding school in Peekskill, New York. In its first season, the show introduces a character played by Geri Jewell, an actress with cerebral palsy. She is the first performer with a disability to have a regular role on a primetime series.

MATTHEW: 1981.

ALL: 1981.

ZAZEL: I receive a merit scholarship to study ballet at Alvin Ailey. I get through the brutal discipline of ballet with the help of a very funny guy named Barry who is from Montserrat. Soon, I am dancing and touring with Alvin Ailey's second company.

BLAIR: 1981.

ALL: 1981.

JOSH: My mother is putting me to bed. We say the Sh'ma together.

(Vivian and Josh say the Hebrew prayer.)

We never want to leave each other. My father says:

MATTHEW: "Elena, let the boy go to sleep."

JOSH: This memory is precious to me. It is one of the few I have of my mother not totally debilitated by multiple sclerosis.

CHRISTOPHER: 1981.

ALL: 1981.

ZAZEL: Washington, D.C.

MONIQUE: I am cast as Chava in *Fiddler on the Roof*. I am a very sloppy signer. The sign master tells me:

JOSH: "Monique, no one in their right mind would pay to see you perform because no one will understand you."

MONIQUE: This hurts at first, but I realize he is right. Under his mentorship, I learn how to sign clearly. Now my performing skills can be seen.

MATTHEW: 1981.

ALL: 1981.

JOSH: Michigan.

ZAZEL: I leave Ailey to study dance at the University of Michigan. At Michigan my style is seen as ethnic, passionate, too emotional, and coming from Ailey doesn't help. Viola Farber is the choreographer in residence. Her temperature is subarctic compared to Ailey. It's cool with a capital "C." I am never picked to be in her work. I feel like an outsider.

MATTHEW: 1984.

ALL: 1984.

JOSH: My mother's condition now requires that she use a walker in the apartment and a wheelchair outside. Tremors prevent her from feeding herself and there is a commode next to the bed. My mother knows—we all know—that life as she has lived it will never return. I am six years old.

MONIQUE: 1984.

ALL: 1984.

CHRISTOPHER: I am born three months premature. I weigh two and a half pounds. I can't breathe on my own. Shortly after my birth I have a massive brain hemorrhage. The doctors tell my parents:

ZAZEL: "You should consider letting him die. He is unlikely to live past his first birthday, and if he does, he will probably be a vegetable."

CHRISTOPHER: My parents tell the doctors:

VIVIAN: "Do everything you can to save him. If there is only a five percent chance he can live, who says he can't be in that five percent?"

JOSH: 1984.

ALL: 1984.

CHRISTOPHER: I am baptized in the hospital and given last rites. My parents are told the hospital needs a name to put on the death certificate. My mother names me Christopher because it has "Christ" in it and she hopes someone upstairs will cut me a break.

ZAZEL: 1984.

ALL: 1984.

JOSH: My mother's anger about her disability is driving my parents apart. They go to therapy. The therapist says:

MATTHEW: "Just give him a smile, Elena. Start there."

JOSH: But my father is an easy target for her rage.

MATTHEW: 1984.

ALL: 1984.

CHRISTOPHER: I am in the intensive care unit for three months. One day a doctor says to my mom:

MONIQUE: "You know, if he survives you can't let this affect his life. You have to let him fall and kiss the dog and eat dirt just like every other kid does."

ZAZEL: 1985.

ALL: 1985.

JOSH: The moment my mother feared most has arrived. My father is leaving. My father and I are both crying, but my mother sits in bed silent and rigid. She will never know intimacy again. I will become all she has left. And the door closes. And I am left on the inside, with her, with her slow death, looking out.

CHRISTOPHER: 1986.

ALL: 1986.

BLAIR: Flushing, Queens.

MONIQUE: I am studying dance with Merce Cunningham. I stay with a friend in Flushing. Flushing is where New York's Koreatown is. I didn't even know there was a Koreatown! Everyone there assumes I am Korean. It's strange. I was raised by white Mennonite parents in Lancaster, Pennsylvania. I have never felt culturally Asian. Now, for the first time, I begin to understand this is part of my identity, too.

(All clap two times.)

JOSH: 1986.

ALL: 1986.

MATTHEW: The International Center for the Disabled and NYU Medical Center decide to start a joint program for adolescents with learning disabilities. I am recommended to lead the program, but there is hesitation. Finally I ask my boss what's going on:

VIVIAN: "Matthew, your work is outstanding. It is not about your work or your qualifications."

MATTHEW: "Well then, what's it about?"

VIVIAN: "The medical director is concerned your disability will traumatize the youth. That's why you won't be leading the program."

MATTHEW: It is my first experience of prejudice in the workplace. I will never forget this painful and sobering experience.

ZAZEL: 1986.

ALL: 1986.

JOSH: I want to crawl inside my mother, to imagine what she imagines, to feel what she feels. I want to send my spirit to be her companion. If I can do this, maybe I can ease her profound loneliness. Years later I will understand that this loneliness is mine as well as hers, and that my identification with my mother is way too close.

VIVIAN: 1987.

ALL: 1987.

BLAIR: My dad is a judge. He teaches me about justice and how to take action to change the world. If I think something is unfair, he says:

ZAZEL: "WRITE A LETTER!"

BLAIR: "But, Dad . . ."

MATTHEW: "Listen, Blair, you can complain, but not for too long, because then it is just noise. If you want change, you must *act*."

(All clap two times.)

MONIQUE: 1988.

ALL: 1988.

JOSH: I am ten years old. I am at sleep-away camp. I receive a letter from my mother. At the bottom there is a postscript. It says:

ZAZEL: "Dear Josh, my name is Anita. I am your mother's new live-in nurse."

JOSH: Anita and I will share a tiny bedroom separated only by a curtain for the next eight years. She is a Pentecostal Christian from the West Indies with very different values than mine.

CHRISTOPHER: 1988.

ALL: 1988.

ZAZEL: Washington, D.C.

MONIQUE: Gallaudet University is the only university in the world for deaf and hard of hearing students, but it has never had a deaf president. Students print fliers that read:

ZAZEL: "It's time! In 1842, a Catholic became president of Notre Dame."

JOSH: "It's time! In 1875, a woman became president of Wellesley College."

BLAIR: "It's time! In 1886, a Jew became president of Yeshiva University."

CHRISTOPHER: "It's time! In 1926, an African American became president of Howard University."

MONIQUE: ". . . and in 1988, the Gallaudet University presidency belongs to a deaf person."

MATTHEW: 1988.

ALL: 1988.

MONIQUE: The trustees of Gallaudet pick another hearing president. The students are shocked. The president of the board declares:

VIVIAN: "The deaf are not yet ready to function in the hearing world."

MONIQUE: The students take over the university amid national media coverage. Their protests succeed. I. King Jordan becomes the first deaf president of Gallaudet University. It is a watershed moment for the deaf community.

(All clap three times.)

BLAIR: 1989.

ALL: 1989.

CHRISTOPHER: Cerebral palsy causes the muscles in my legs to be too tight and keeps my bones from growing straight. My feet are beginning to point backwards. I can walk, but only with crutches and braces for support. My mom says to me:

ZAZEL: "Christopher, there is a surgery you can have to help you walk better, but it will be painful and you will be in the hospital for a long time. Do you want to do it?"

CHRISTOPHER: I want to do the surgery. I really want to be able to walk like my older brother, Vinnie. It will be the first of many, many surgeries. I am five years old.

MATTHEW: 1989.

ALL: 1989.

JOSH: My mother joins the MS Society, but her increasing bitterness and anger are in opposition to the community there. What would have happened if she had reached out, had searched for a connection to others that helped her transcend her isolation, which connected her to a sense of something greater than herself?

MONIQUE: 1989.

ALL: 1989.

ZAZEL: My friend, Barry, from Alvin Ailey is on an international dance tour. While in South Africa, he is in a car accident. He is rushed to a hospital, but because he is black, the hospital won't treat him. He is paralyzed for life.

VIVIAN: 1989.

ALL: 1989.

MONIQUE: I am attending Deaf Way, an international festival on deaf culture in D.C. I meet deaf groups from Israel and Norway and

Turkey. It is an interesting challenge to see how international sign languages differ from ASL. For example, this is the sign for "thank you" in ASL. *(She demonstrates)* But this is the sign for "thank you" in Turkish sign. *(She demonstrates)* One night, we all end up at a Korean restaurant. I have never been to one before. I grew up around Pennsylvania food:

VIVIAN: scrapple,

BLAIR: sausage,

CHRISTOPHER: bologna.

MONIQUE: Any vegetables we cooked, we cooked until they were dead. My first response to Korean food—

ALL *(Speaking and signing in ASL)*: SPICY!

JOSH: 1989.

ALL: 1989.

CHRISTOPHER: After my surgeries, I go to physical therapy five times a week. I use my imagination to escape the pain. I pretend that I am Peter Pan and can fly away to Neverland. My therapist, Donna Piccone, suggests that my mom send me to theater camp.

BLAIR: 1990.

ALL: 1990.

CHRISTOPHER: I am six years old. I go to theater camp and love it. At first, I can't walk backwards with my crutches. But if you can't walk backwards, you can't take a bow. When I hear the applause for the first time, I learn to walk backwards very quickly! Later, the camp director casts me in his professional production of *Peter Pan*. It is my first paying theater job.

JOSH: 1990.

ALL: 1990.

BLAIR: The Americans with Disabilities Act is signed into law. It protects people with disabilities from discrimination in the workplace, in housing, in public accommodations, in transportation and in telecommunications.

ZAZEL: This didn't happen because Congress just woke up one day and decided to pass it. It is because people with disabilities organized and took action—just like people who want change of any kind anywhere.

(All clap ten times.
    The Norwegian incantation begins to play. The ensemble freezes as the lights fade down to a silhouette. It is an interval of stillness. Then the music fades and lights slowly come back up.)

JOSH: 1990.

BLAIR: 1990.

ALL: 1990.

CHRISTOPHER: It is time for me to start kindergarten. The other parents say:

ZAZEL: "Why can't he go to school with his own kind?"

CHRISTOPHER: On the playground, parents pull their kids away from me. My mom says:

BLAIR: "You know, you can't catch cerebral palsy."

CHRISTOPHER: Thanks to the Americans with Disabilities Act, it is illegal for them to refuse to let me attend this school.

(All clap two times.)

ALL: 1990.

JOSH: My father calls regularly to see how things are—to ask if we need any help—but little by little I shut him out. I don't want anyone to think I can't handle it. I tell him:

CHRISTOPHER: "I can do it. Everything is okay. We are fine."

ALL: 1991.

BLAIR: New York City.

MONIQUE: I am attending NYU. Now, because of the ADA, I have interpreters for all my classes. What a difference from when I was a kid. Now, I can enjoy learning.

(All clap two times.)

ALL: 1991.

ZAZEL: In the last decade, my career has taken off. I am in a regional tour of *The Wiz*, I dance in musicals, I sign with Wilhelmina Models, Inc. and I get two covers of *Essence* magazine. Then I hit the jackpot and get a national commercial for McDonald's. I join the Screen Actors Guild. Life is good.

(All clap.)

CHRISTOPHER AND BLAIR: 1991.

MATTHEW: NYU Medical Center.

VIVIAN: After working here for over ten years, I learn that men in the same executive positions are making twenty thousand dollars a year more than I am. As a woman, there's a very fine line you must walk in a man's world. Work hard, have ambition, insist on excellence and you're too aggressive; show your softer side and you're too emotional, too weak.

MONIQUE AND JOSH: 1992.

BLAIR: I am a senior in high school. I am the number one singles player on the tennis team and I'm also on the undefeated basketball team. I decide to attend Hartwick College, a small liberal arts college in the Catskill Mountains.

ALL: 1992.

CHRISTOPHER: I am in second grade. I come home from school crying because the neighborhood boys made fun of me. My mom says:

BLAIR: "Look, there are always going to be bad things in life, so don't feel sorry for yourself, because it can always be worse. And if the kids make fun of you, just tell them:

CHRISTOPHER: "'At least I can go to therapy and have surgery, and get better, but you will always be a jerk!'"

(All clap.)

MATTHEW: 1992.

ZAZEL: 1992.

JOSH AND MONIQUE: 1992.

CHRISTOPHER: November 15, 1992.

BLAIR: I am a freshman in college. I am on my way back to Hartwick after a weekend away with some friends. We are three exits from campus. It's about six in the evening. It is dark. The weather is bad, the road is icy. Suddenly, we skid and veer out of control. The car flips and rolls over and over.

VIVIAN: One,

JOSH: two,

ZAZEL: three eternities pass.

BLAIR: I am on the ground away from the car. My arm is on the guardrail. My legs are not moving. It is really, really quiet. I can hear my friends screaming in the distance, but where I am it is strangely peaceful.

VIVIAN: 1992.

JOSH: 1992.

ALL: 1992.

ZAZEL: Bassett Memorial Hospital.

CHRISTOPHER: Cooperstown, New York.

BLAIR: Five days after the accident, I have my first surgery. I have:

MONIQUE: a broken collar bone,

CHRISTOPHER: three broken ribs,

ZAZEL: a collapsed lung,

MONIQUE: and three fractured vertebrae.

BLAIR: After the surgery, I feel fire in my legs—tingling and pins and needles. I think I am getting the feeling back. I think I can move my toes. A young resident comes into the room to show me my X-rays. He says:

CHRISTOPHER: "You have three fractured vertebrae: here, here and here—the T-11, L-1, and T-12. If it had just been the T-11 and L-1, you would be able to walk again. But the T-12 makes it impossible."

BLAIR: I say, "Can I still have sex?"

CHRISTOPHER: "Yes."

BLAIR: "Can I still have kids?"

CHRISTOPHER: "Yes."

BLAIR: "Okay, then I'm cool." What else can you say? I am eighteen years old.

(*All clap.*)

ALL: 1992.

VIVIAN: Scranton, Pennsylvania.

BLAIR: I spend eight weeks in rehab. It is not fun and the food sucks. I notice there are no other women in chairs on my floor. Kim, one of the nurses, looks out for me. She has had her own car accident. Her face has been reconstructed. She is always laughing. She says to me:

ZAZEL: "Look, Blair, you have to have fun here. I'll help you. Have fun or you will go crazy."

BLAIR: She shows me how to cut pancakes into circles and . . .

CHRISTOPHER: One.

ALL: Splat!

JOSH: Two.

ALL: Splat!

MATTHEW: Three.

ALL: Splat!

BLAIR: . . . fling them on the walls, where they stick forever. Kim gets me through a lot of b.s. and pain while I am at rehab.

ALL: 1993.

JOSH: February 1993.

BLAIR: I leave rehab and go home to Poughkeepsie. After the accident, I got so many flowers at the hospital that the florist refused to deliver any more. Now, everyone has moved on. Now, I have to get on with my life.

MATTHEW AND MONIQUE: 1993.

CHRISTOPHER: There is a bully that hangs out in the boys' bathroom. Whenever he sees me he says:

MATTHEW: "I don't like you. You look funny. I'm going to beat you up."

CHRISTOPHER: One day he threatens me and I beat him with my crutches. I get called to the principal's office. I have never been in trouble before in my whole life. I start to cry.

JOSH: "My mother is going to kill me!"

CHRISTOPHER: The principal looks very grave.

VIVIAN: "Chris, you know we don't allow fighting. Why did you do this?"

JOSH: "I had to—he called me a cripple!"

CHRISTOPHER: I do not get in trouble after all. I have the uncomfortable realization that I can sometimes use my disability to my own advantage. I am nine years old.

ALL: 1993.

JOSH: I hate sports. I love theater. I am painfully aware of the ways I am not like other boys. "Manliness" is a responsibility I am afraid I can't live up to. Anita tries to instill a more traditional model of manliness. When she sees me knitting she says:

ZAZEL: "It's time to put away those girl things and play with men things."

(All clap.)

VIVIAN AND CHRISTOPHER: 1993.

BLAIR: My dad finds out about a wheelchair basketball team nearby. I am excited to check it out, but when I get there I see only hardened older men—mostly veterans. I am intimidated. There is no one my age and no one my gender. I decide not to go back.

ALL: 1993.

MONIQUE: April 1993.

BLAIR: I am working in my father's law office as a receptionist. One day after work, there is a car in the parking lot with hand controls. My dad hands me the keys and says:

MATTHEW: "So I'll see you at home."

BLAIR: "But, Dad, I only watched videos in rehab and never really drove! I don't know if I can do it!"

MATTHEW: "You can figure it out. I'll see you at home."

BLAIR: From that day on, I drive everywhere. That car gives me my freedom.

(*All clap two times.*)

ALL: 1993.

CHRISTOPHER: September 1993.

BLAIR: Hartwick promises they will make the campus accessible for me, but when I get back to school the construction isn't finished yet. Everyone wants me to stay, but I just can't. I realize I never stopped to breathe. I need more time to figure it all out.

CHRISTOPHER AND JOSH: 1994.

MONIQUE: Los Angeles.

MATTHEW: The Moebius Syndrome Foundation holds its first conference. I attend the first gathering in L.A. When I walk into the ballroom, I am astonished to see one hundred and two people affected by Moebius syndrome. I feel the earth shake beneath my feet. I have finally come home.

(*All clap three times.*)

ALL: 1994.

ZAZEL: New York City.

MATTHEW: I go to the first meeting of a support group called Inner Faces. When I arrive I realize it is a meeting for a theater group. I am terrified! I'm trying to make a quick getaway when a woman comes up to me:

MONIQUE: "You're so courageous to come here and not walk away."

MATTHEW: I stay.

ALL: 1994.

MATTHEW: Months later, I step on stage for the first time. I walk off transformed. All my life, people have stared at me without my permission. Now, for the first time, I am choosing to let them stare.

(*All clap ten times.*)

JOSH: Monique?

MONIQUE: Yes, Josh?

JOSH: What do *you* think of when you hear the word "disability"?

MONIQUE: Like many deaf people, I resist the word "disability." I just don't hear. When people learn that I cannot hear, they label me disabled. Conversation is a two-way street. If people lack the ability to adapt to my language, then their lack of flexibility makes me disabled.

(All clap two times.)

ALL: 1995.

JOSH: My grandmother dies. Although she and my mother had a contentious relationship, my grandmother supported both of us. I still visit my father regularly but I am now completely alone with my mother.

ALL: 1995.

CHRISTOPHER: I still want to walk like my brother, Vinnie. I have more surgery. A metal frame is put on the outside of my leg with four bolts going into the bone. I am covered in gauze, with metal everywhere. I look like Frankenstein. When Vinnie sees me he freaks out:

JOSH: "What did you do to him? Can't you see he is in pain? Why can't you just leave him alone?"

CHRISTOPHER: This is the first time I realize how much my brother really cares about me. I am eleven years old.

MATTHEW AND BLAIR: 1995.

JOSH: Seattle, Washington.

VIVIAN: I am the Chief Operating Officer of Harborview Medical Center. Tensions build between the Minority Affairs Council and the administration. I am asked to act as the liaison to see what can be done to improve relations. One problem is that minorities mainly hold low-paying jobs:

ZAZEL: housekeeping,

MONIQUE: food service,

CHRISTOPHER: maintenance.

VIVIAN: It is a sure way to create resentment. I work to recruit and train minority workers for better positions.

CHRISTOPHER AND JOSH: 1995.

BLAIR: I still haven't met another woman in a chair. I still feel alone. I get an invitation from the American Paralysis Association for a benefit at Tavern on the Green. It is nearly Christmas—everything is lit up and beautiful. When I see all these rich people supporting the Spinal Cord Injury Association, I realize there is something in this that is much bigger than me. I realize I can be my own representative in this.

(All clap two times.)

MONIQUE AND JOSH: 1995.
JOSH: I learn to decipher my mother's needs as she grows more and
more sick:
CHRISTOPHER: "Raise the blinds."
MONIQUE: "Lower the blinds."
CHRISTOPHER: "Change the channel."
MONIQUE: "Bring me some water."
JOSH: I learn to interpret a near constant ask of "favors" to mean:
ZAZEL: "I'm lonely, come talk to me."
JOSH: I have to understand that
ZAZEL: "I need you to do this for me"
JOSH: is as close as she can come to saying:
ZAZEL: "I need you."
ALL: 1995.
ZAZEL: Queens, New York.
BLAIR: LaGuardia Community College.
MATTHEW: The Office for Students with Disabilities is created. I am
hired to lead it, to be the first director. The goals are:
ZAZEL: to create understanding about the needs of students with
disabilities,
MONIQUE: to help them academically,
CHRISTOPHER: to make clear to everyone that "disability" does not
mean "stupid."

(All clap.)

ALL: 1996.
MATTHEW: I am in a PBS documentary entitled *Face: A Portrait*. It
is shown at a Long Island high school. Afterwards, a student
bursts into tears. She says:
ZAZEL: "I was worried my boyfriend wouldn't want to go out with me
because I have a pimple. Now I realize how petty my concerns
are. You are the one struggling with real life issues."
MATTHEW: Her outburst is like the bolt of lightning in Michelangelo's Sistine Chapel when God and Adam touch. It is one of
the most powerful experiences of my life. In some way, I have
never felt closer to another human being. I seek that moment
again and again every day.

(All clap two times.)

ALL: 1996.

ZAZEL: "Joshua, you are your mother's one happiness. You are the reason why she is alive."

JOSH: I feel like a fraud. I want less and less to be with my mother. I know I can't save her. I want to get away from that visceral decay, the bedsores, the rancid stench of sickness, but her presence permeates every inch of our tiny apartment. I go to my dad's after school when he's not there, just to be alone. I need privacy. Alone, in private, is the only place I can have my own emotions, my own needs. I am seventeen years old.

ALL: 1997.

VIVIAN: I receive an e-mail from the President of the Minority Affairs Council:

BLAIR: "Martin Luther King, Jr.'s dream of justice and equality is also our dream. The steps taken by Harborview Medical Center have brought us closer to this dream, in large part because of your support and guidance. Please accept our gratitude."

VIVIAN: This is one of the proudest moments of my career.

(All clap two times)

MATTHEW AND CHRISTOPHER: 1997.

JOSH: I know I have to leave. I know I have to go away for college. I have to begin the process of separating to live. I know that my mother is dying. It is painful, but I shut the pain inside and do not share it with anyone.

ALL: 1998.

MONIQUE: I try to get my agent in New York to send me out for parts that don't require speaking, but they only want to send me out for parts that call for deaf actors. They don't know how to market me. It drives me nuts. Don't people know there is so much more to acting than just dialogue?

ALL: 1998.

BLAIR: New York City.

ZAZEL: During a slow period, I get a temp job at Macy's as a special events coordinator. While I'm working, a strange feeling rushes from my stomach to my head, like a flash—then it is gone. Six months later, fatigue kicks in. The flashes start again. What is going on?

MATTHEW AND BLAIR: 1998.

VIVIAN: Wesleyan University, Connecticut.

JOSH: At Wesleyan, I find my calling as a theater director and I come out as a gay man. Coming out takes the pressure off the manliness game. Now I can explore myriad colors of gender expression.

(All clap two times.)

ALL: 1998.

ZAZEL: Dutchess Community College, Poughkeepsie.

BLAIR: I am back in school again. I need an elective, and the counselor suggests taking an acting class. When I show up on the first day, the teacher, Steve Press, gives me this look like:

CHRISTOPHER: "What am I going to do with you?"

BLAIR: I feel his look and think:

ZAZEL: Forget it, I'm out of here!

BLAIR: But then he says:

CHRISTOPHER: "Well, I don't know what's going to happen, but please stay in the class and we'll figure it out together."

BLAIR: We have to get on stage and introduce ourselves. When I get up there, something magical happens. I feel the wood under my chair, the lights, the warmth all around me. For just one second, I feel complete. I say:

ZAZEL: "My name is Blair Wing and I am an actress."

(All clap ten times.)

MATTHEW: Blair?

BLAIR: Yes, Matthew?

MATTHEW: What do *you* think of when you hear the word "disability"?

BLAIR: *Dis*-ability. At first it means a "dis," like when I was growing up, my friends and I would "dis" each other. Then I look closer and see "lack of ability." But I can accomplish more in one day with a smile than most people, because I enjoy *doing*. I prefer the term "mixed ability." It puts everyone on an even playing field.

(All clap two times.)

VIVIAN: Josh?

JOSH: Yes, Vivian?

VIVIAN: What do *you* think of when you hear the word "disability"?

JOSH: Disabled, not unable. My mother said that frequently. I think of a physical condition that threatens to obscure the beauty inside. Paradoxically, I think disability has the potential to shed light on what it is to be human—the courage it takes sometimes simply to live.

(All clap two times.)

ALL: 1999.

CHRISTOPHER: I am fifteen years old. I am trying to decide if I should have more surgery. It is painful and disrupts my life, but I am also determined to do as much as I can. My mom says:

VIVIAN: "Christopher, I don't want to look at you when you are twenty-one and think that there was more I could have done for you."

CHRISTOPHER: After one last surgery, I am walking without any support. I have reached the goal I set out for myself. I feel totally free.

(All clap three times.)

ALL: 2000.

ZAZEL: I'm writing a check and notice my handwriting looks different. Later that day, I go to an audition. When it's my turn the director says:

MONIQUE: "State your name, please."

ZAZEL: A bolt rushes through my body. Then a huge bolt crashes through me.

MONIQUE: "State your name, please."

ZAZEL: Everybody is looking at me. I'm standing there like a fool, smiling and unable to speak.

MONIQUE: "State your name, please."

ZAZEL: Then it vanishes. What is going on?

CHRISTOPHER AND MATTHEW: 2000.

JOSH: My mother is now completely paralyzed. She is blind, her skin is greasy, her tongue is thick, her hair is thin. I barely recognize her as my mother. I don't want to look at her. I don't want to be near her. I feel terrible guilt about this. Profound illness and its proximity to death frighten me. I am twenty-two years old.

ALL: 2000.

MONIQUE: Many hearing people don't understand how a deaf person can work in a hearing environment. They aren't willing to try and figure it out. Of course no one is going to say to you:

ZAZEL: "Well, no, we are not going to hire you because you are deaf."

MONIQUE: I am looking for a retail job. At Pier 1, they are really friendly; they make a big deal of being nice to me. At Williams-Sonoma, they are rude and irritable. Strangely, I never hear from Pier 1 again, but Williams-Sonoma hires me. Still, sometimes I wonder if they only hired me to be politically correct.

ALL: 2000.

MATTHEW: Sometimes it's easier to walk than to hail a cab. One night, thirteen cabs in a row abandon me in the snow.

(All clap.)

ALL: 2000.

JOSH: Maybe you have Epstein-Barr.

VIVIAN: Maybe it's early menopause.

BLAIR: Let's do an AIDS test.

CHRISTOPHER: Maybe it's a sinus infection.

ZAZEL: I start getting killer headaches and nausea. The flashes come and go—sometimes strong, sometimes weak. What should I do?

ALL: 2001.

JOSH: Pursuing a career in theater means paying dues and working odd jobs. I am working as a waiter in SoHo. One day, I get a phone call at work. It's Anita:

ZAZEL: "Can you come to the hospital?"

CHRISTOPHER: "I'm working. Do you need me to come?"

ZAZEL: "Come now."

JOSH: When I get to the hospital, Anita and I hug. I think I should hold my mother's hand right now. In a minute, they are going to take her away and put her in a box and I won't be able to hold her hand ever again.

(All clap.)

ALL: 2001.

JOSH: A lot of people come to the funeral. Where were they when she was alive? After the funeral, I sever all ties with my mother's family, who were never there for her or for me. I never see them again.

ALL: 2002.

ZAZEL: My sister, Cathy, takes me to St. Barnabus Hospital in New Jersey to get an MRI.

VIVIAN: One,

JOSH: two,

MATTHEW: three eternities pass. The results come back:

BLAIR: "Okay, you have a brain tumor behind your left ear. It's a problematic operation. Most likely you will have facial paralysis. There could be slurred speech, and it could cause blindness or death. The good news is the tumor is benign."

CHRISTOPHER: "Oh, we have to ask, do you have insurance?"

(All clap.)

ALL: 2002.

ZAZEL: The tumor diagnosis is on December 27. My health insurance expires on December 30. My dad has passed. My mom is eighty-two. I don't want to go into my savings. I am desperate.

ALL: 2002.

ZAZEL: I call The Actors Fund and ask:

BLAIR: "I'm having surgery and I need help with my health insurance. Can you help me?"

ZAZEL: They pay for my health insurance, which covers everything. Bless them. I promise to pay my union dues forever.

(All clap three times.)

BLAIR: 2003.

CHRISTOPHER: 2003.

BLAIR: 2003.

CHRISTOPHER: January 10, 2003.

ZAZEL: The brain surgery takes eleven and a half hours. When I wake up, the first thing I ask is:

BLAIR: "Can I see a mirror?"

ZAZEL: The nurse says:

MONIQUE: "I don't think so. I don't think so."

ZAZEL: I look in the mirror anyway. My face is not paralyzed, but I am seeing double. My ex-boyfriend—and I mean *ex*—comes to see me. I say:

BLAIR: "This is the guy who screwed me up."

ZAZEL: He says:

CHRISTOPHER: "She hasn't changed."

(All clap.)

ALL: 2003.

ZAZEL: The surgery leaves me with paralysis on my right side. I'm in rehab. I go for occupational therapy, physical therapy, speech therapy. They want to know if I'm suicidal. I say:

BLAIR: "No, I want to catch the next sale at Macy's!"

(All clap.)

ALL: 2003.

ZAZEL: The food in rehab sucks, but my mother brings me jerk chicken, rice and peas, and salt fish and dumplings. My room smells like a restaurant.

ALL: 2003. Rules, rules, rules!

CHRISTOPHER: "You're not allowed out of your wheelchair!"

BLAIR: "You can't go to the bathroom by yourself!"

ZAZEL: I don't like rules. I'm a dancer—I'm hyper. I start doing stretches in my wheelchair. I push myself physically. The therapists think I'm crazy, but I'm used to pain—ballet is all about pain! My recovery is quick, but my right foot remains paralyzed. I am determined to dance again!

(All clap.)

ALL: 2003.

BLAIR: I am going to Ohio State for my MFA in acting. I am one of ten students in the program. When the first show is cast, I am the only one not auditioned. Then the wardrobe assistant says to me:

ZAZEL: "Oh, they pre-cast you. You are going to play the old lady in the wheelchair. She stays on the porch for the whole show. They didn't know what else to do with you."

BLAIR: I am really upset, but I don't want to make a big scene. After all, I just got here. I don't want to rock the boat.

ALL: 2003.

ZAZEL: My friend Barry, who is paralyzed, lives his life fully. He choreographs from his wheelchair. When Barry hears about my tumor, he encourages me to go back to school and to get involved with disability-support organizations. He shows me that life doesn't have to stop.

ALL: 2003.

CHRISTOPHER: I am applying for college. I know I want to study acting. My first choice is Rutgers. At the audition I am asked:

BLAIR: "Why do you walk funny?"

JOSH: "Well, I have cerebral palsy, and it does affect my walk, but it has never stopped me from doing what I want to do."

ZAZEL: "Hmmm, well, we have never had anyone like that in our program. Oh, wait! We did have that one guy who had a wooden leg."

JOSH: "Well, I don't have a wooden leg."

CHRISTOPHER: I do not get accepted to the program.

ALL: 2003.

JOSH: Another bond my mother and I share is that we both have childhood diabetes. It's a chronic disease. It is affecting my vision. When I go to the eye doctor, I am overcome with emotion. I look around and see:

VIVIAN: a woman with dark glasses accompanied by her husband,

MATTHEW: a woman accompanied by a nurse's aid,

MONIQUE: a woman with no one at all.

JOSH: I fear my eyes—these windows to my soul—will seal shut, leaving me on the inside, in the dark, alone. How will anyone ever find me in there if they can't get in?

ALL: 2003.

BLAIR: I am meeting my boyfriend's parents for the first time. I am a little nervous. I wait outside the pizza restaurant while my boyfriend tells them I am coming in. When he comes out, he has a funny look on his face. He says:

CHRISTOPHER: "Now, Blair, you have to promise to be nice."

ZAZEL: "Of course I'll be nice. Why? What did they say?"

CHRISTOPHER: "Well, my mom asked how you can possibly have sex and have children if you are in a wheelchair."

BLAIR: I roll into the restaurant and right up to his mom:

ZAZEL: "Hi. I'm Blair. It's nice to meet you. Is there anything you want to ask me? Feel free!"

MONIQUE: There is a long awkward pause. Then she says:

VIVIAN: "Um, so . . . what kind of pizza do you like?"

(All clap.)

ALL: 2004.

JOSH: Montserrat, West Indies.

ZAZEL: I've been going to Montserrat, my mother's homeland, since I was four years old, but this time it is different. This time I have a "disability." When people see me walking down the street they treat me like a freak. They say:

BLAIR: "Why you walk wit stick?"

CHRISTOPHER: "What's wrong wit your foot?"

ZAZEL: If you have a disability in Montserrat, you are supposed to go into hiding and close the door. I refuse to do this. Instead, I parade all over the island in colorful halters and bikinis to show people you don't have to hide.

(*All clap two times.*)

VIVIAN AND JOSH: 2004.

CHRISTOPHER: Ohio.

BLAIR: Both elevators in my apartment building are broken. If the elevators are out, it means I can't leave the building. I complain to the management, but they don't do anything. Days go by. I am furious. I remember my dad's words:

ZAZEL: "Write a letter!"

MATTHEW: "Don't just complain!"

ALL (*Speaking and signing in ASL*): "TAKE ACTION!"

BLAIR: So I write a letter and—miracle of miracles—the civil rights office agrees to mediate a hearing. I win my case and actually see real change. I'm proud that I stood up for myself and actually righted a wrong.

(*All clap ten times.*

The Norwegian incantation begins to play. The ensemble freezes as the lights fade down to a silhouette. It is an interval of stillness. Then the music fades and lights slowly come back up.)

CHRISTOPHER: 2004.

VIVIAN AND BLAIR: 2004.

ALL: 2004.

JOSH: I meet a guy named Rick in a gay bar. He feels kind and safe but I am terrified of opening up to him. All my life, I was the caregiver, not the one who was cared for. I challenge myself not to run away from him.

ALL: 2004.

JOSH: A few weeks later I tell my therapist about my fears. She says:

ZAZEL: "Can you imagine him being inside there with you? Can you imagine trusting him enough to do that?"

JOSH: Rick and I fall in love.

(*All clap two times.*)

ALL: 2004.

ZAZEL: Despite my disability, my agency still wants me as a client. They send me to audition for a Coca-Cola commercial. When I get there the director says:

CHRISTOPHER: "Here's the setup: You see your kid across the street and you're really happy to see him. You run to him and hug him."

ZAZEL: I think to myself:

BLAIR: Oh, great, they want me to run.

ZAZEL: I don't get the job. After all, there's no such thing as a disabled mom in the world, is there?

(All clap.)

ALL: 2005.

CHRISTOPHER: July 2005.

MATTHEW: Tuscany, Italy.

VIVIAN: My husband, Jeffrey, and I rent a house in Tuscany. It is paradise. One morning I am taking pictures of sunflowers—sunflowers as far the eye can see. Suddenly, I feel as if someone is coming over my shoulder, but there's no one there. Later that day, I see a veil of dots floating in my right eye. What's going on?

ALL: 2005.

VIVIAN: The next day, we drive to Florence. The doctors aren't sure what it is. Tuscany is so beautiful, we stay two more weeks. It's a mistake, but we don't know it yet.

ALL: 2005.

BLAIR: New York Eye and Ear Hospital.

VIVIAN: A retinal surgeon says:

ZAZEL: "You have seven tears on your retina."

CHRISTOPHER: "You have seven tears on your retina."

JOSH: "You have seven tears on your retina."

VIVIAN: I have multiple surgeries and different treatments. I have to sleep on a special bed, face down, my face poking through a hole, for months. It is torture. None of the treatments work.

(All clap.)

ALL: 2005.

BLAIR: It seems like there are only two possible representations of women in chairs on TV. The first is no representation at all. The second one goes something like this:

ZAZEL: "Next on *Lifetime Original Movie!*"

CHRISTOPHER: "Her boyfriend pushed her down a hill!"

VIVIAN: "They had too much to drink!"

MATTHEW: "Now, she is . . ."

ZAZEL: "CONFINED TO A WHEELCHAIR FOREVER!"

CHRISTOPHER: "Will she ever be independent?"

MONIQUE: "Wait!"

ZAZEL: "She moved her toe!"

ALL *(Speaking and signing in ASL)*: "It's a miracle!"

BLAIR: Okay, that was *not* written by a woman in a chair!

(All clap.)

ALL: 2005.

BLAIR: My nephew, Isaiah, says to me:

CHRISTOPHER: "Aunt Blair, when will there be people in wheelchairs on TV like all the other people on TV? When will *you* be on TV?"

BLAIR: I say:

ZAZEL: "We're working on it."

BLAIR: I am accepted into a PhD program in London. I will write my dissertation on the underrepresentation of women with mixed abilities in the media.

(All clap.)

ALL: 2006.

JOSH: My mother has been gone for five years. One night, I dream I am a child standing in front of a glowing boulder that I know is my mother. I can still feel the tenderness between me and this glowing stone—the love and care and happiness. I miss my mother.

ALL: 2006.

BLAIR: I hear about an open audition for a major network TV show. They are looking for actresses who use wheelchairs. I am really psyched. I drive all the way from Ohio to New York for the audition. Afterwards, my agent tells me I didn't get the part:

ZAZEL: "They said you're too pretty—you don't look disabled enough."

BLAIR: A few weeks later, I see the episode on TV. The part went to an actress without a disability. How is it possible that I do not look disabled enough, but she does?

(All clap.)

ALL: 2006.

VIVIAN: Rowan University.

CHRISTOPHER: My theater professor, Simone Federman, says to me:

ZAZEL: "There is an organization called VSA arts. They are starting an apprenticeship for artists with disabilities at the Williamstown Theatre Festival this summer. You should apply."

CHRISTOPHER: I put in the application and hope for the best. I really, really want this. Christopher Reeve was an apprentice at Williamstown and it launched his career. A few weeks later I get a call:

BLAIR: "Christopher, great news! You are the inaugural VSA arts apprentice. You are going to Williamstown."

(All clap two times.)

ALL: 2006.

MATTHEW: Every day I come home from work and greet my neighbors. They greet me back, but there is one neighbor who will do anything—*anything*—to avoid me. I wonder what it would take for him to see me as the same human being he is?

(All clap.)

ALL: 2006.

MONIQUE: Nowadays, everyone is text-messaging, instant-messaging and e-mailing. People are on MySpace and Facebook. Technology makes it easier for deaf people to communicate with the hearing world, and vice versa. The best thing about it is that everyone uses it, so no one says:

BLAIR: "Oh, that technology is something special just for deaf people."

MONIQUE: Everyone is addicted to instant-messaging. Just ask a teenager!

(All clap.)

ALL: 2006.

BLAIR: Tuscany, Italy.

VIVIAN: We have returned to Italy, but something starts to go wrong again. I am looking at the stars that fill the night sky. Suddenly, lights start flashing in my left eye. I don't tell Jeffrey, hoping it will go away.

ALL *(Speaking and then signing in ASL)*: Time passes.

VIVIAN: I am terrified. I finally tell Jeffrey what's going on. He puts his head in his hands, then he says:

JOSH: "Pack your bags. We're out of here."

(All clap.)

CHRISTOPHER: 2006.

MONIQUE: 2006.

ALL: 2006.

JOSH: The same night.

VIVIAN: Jeffrey manages to get two tickets from Rome to New York. We drive all night and twenty-four hours later I am in the retinal surgeon's office. He says:

MATTHEW: "We've never seen anything like this."

VIVIAN: Then the nightmare surgeries begin again. I am left with limited vision in my left eye as well. Nothing helps.

(All clap.)

ALL: 2006.

JOSH: Vivian?

VIVIAN: Yes, Josh?

JOSH: What can you see?

VIVIAN: Most people see a friend on a street and recognize their face. They can tell if the person is smiling, sad, happy to see you. I see a person. I can't tell if it's a man or woman or who it is until they are directly in front of me and tell me who they are. I have no peripheral vision and everything is fuzzy. Fortunately, I can still see color.

(All clap.)

ALL: 2007.

JOSH: Growing up with a disabled mother has profoundly influenced my work as a director. My experience having to intuit my mother's unspoken needs is something I draw on whenever I work with actors and the text.

(All clap.)

ALL: 2007.

VIVIAN: I am now legally blind, which means I need special equipment to help me see and read.

BLAIR: A simple battery-operated, hand-held magnifier costs more than six hundred and ninety-five dollars.

MATTHEW: A desktop video reader that lets you to read your mail and newspaper costs more than three thousand dollars.

MONIQUE: A large format program that allows you to use your computer and access the internet costs over six hundred dollars.

VIVIAN: It saddens me that there are many people who can't afford this equipment. A majority of the blind are unemployed.

(All clap.)

ALL: 2007.

BLAIR: I love to travel, but flying is full of unpleasant adventures for me. Imagine showing up at JFK and your wheelchair never left London! Imagine airline staff that refuse to believe you can go to the bathroom by yourself. Imagine a stewardess saying to you:

ZAZEL: "I'm sorry, but you have to sit in the window seat. If there is an emergency, we have to evacuate able-bodied passengers first. You will be in the way."

BLAIR: How would you feel?

(All clap.)

ALL: 2007.

VIVIAN: I was always the go-to, can-do person for everything and everyone. I would cook Thanksgiving dinner for twenty all by myself. All of a sudden, I'm a disabled person. I feel bad. I feel like I'm letting my family down. I ask myself:

ZAZEL: Why did this have to happen to me?

VIVIAN: I worried about breast cancer, heart disease, stroke, anything else, but not this.

(All clap.)

ALL: 2007.

ZAZEL: I teach dance therapy for hospital audiences, for people with developmental disabilities. There's a guy I work with who flirts with me all the time. One day I see him coming down the street with a friend. He sees me, but he walks right past me without saying hello. It's not cool to be talking to a woman with a limp. He would be unmanned.

155

(All clap.)

ALL: 2007.

VIVIAN: It has been hard for Jeffrey, but he treats me as if I have no disability. Some family and friends stop calling. When I need to shop for a gown, the close friend I count on deserts me. Another friend surprises me with her exceptional kindness and loyalty. You never know who is going to be there for you until there is a crisis.

(All clap.)

ALL: 2007.

ZAZEL: I am invited to be the keynote speaker for Long Island University's graduation. The theme of my speech is "Turning Setbacks into Comebacks."

(All clap ten times.)

Chris?

CHRISTOPHER: Yes, Zazel?

ZAZEL: What do *you* think of when you hear the word "disability"?

CHRISTOPHER: Disabled as in "*un*-abled." I never quite understood why it replaced "handicapped," especially since it is so embedded into American culture: handicapped parking, handicapped seating, handicapped bathrooms. Personally, I think handicapped sounds better than disabled. Handicapped suggests you can, but it's a little more difficult, like in horse racing or golf.

(All clap two times.)

ALL: 2007.

VIVIAN: New York City.

BLAIR: I am getting out of my car. People are staring at me. One woman stops and says:

ZAZEL: "Jesus Loves You!"

BLAIR: I don't know why, but I get that a lot. Another man asks if I need help. I say:

MONIQUE: "No, thanks. I'm good."

MATTHEW: "Are you sure?"

BLAIR: He starts walking over to me. This happens a lot, too. I want to scream:

MONIQUE: "How do you think I got here? Do you really think I would have gotten in the car if I couldn't get out again?"

BLAIR: Later my friend José says:

JOSH: "Look, sweetie, this is New York. It's surprising to get people to talk to you at all. They're just trying to be nice."

(All clap.)

ALL: 2007.

VIVIAN: Until you become legally blind, you are not aware how important it is to have steps, raised areas and other obstacles clearly identified. It amazes me how many public staircases do not have a white or yellow strip, particularly on the last step. Most Americans don't have to think about disability, but most Americans will have a disability at some point in their lifetime.

ALL: 2008.

CHRISTOPHER: I get a part in a theater production. All the performers have different disabilities. Everyone is really involved in disability issues and activism, and I feel a little out of place. As someone who grew up post-ADA, I never had to face a lot of issues they had to face. At the talkback an audience member says:

JOSH: "Well, I don't know much about being handicapped but . . ."

(All gasp.)

CHRISTOPHER: They are horrified! Later someone says:

BLAIR: "Can you believe he said that?"

CHRISTOPHER: But this person went out of his way to see this show! He is brave enough to ask a question. Why are we punishing him? I feel like people are so caught up in terminology and political correctness that we are forgetting to talk about the real issues.

(All clap.)

ALL: 2008.

VIVIAN: The writer Elizabeth Kübler-Ross identified five stages of death and dying. In many ways, I feel like I am experiencing all five stages at once:

MONIQUE: denial,

BLAIR: anger,

MATTHEW: bargaining,

CHRISTOPHER: depression,

JOSH: acceptance.

VIVIAN: It took me a while to use my white cane. I was embarrassed. I now view my cane as a companion, who helps me stay independent. I know when I walk down the street with my cane, I am viewed as disabled. My job now is to educate people on how to treat me as a person and not as a disability.

(All clap.)

ALL: 2008.

MONIQUE: I am a Presidential Fellow and adjunct theater professor at Gallaudet University. I am a coach and a counselor for the young people here. Even in 2008, a lot of my students don't have professional, deaf role models. I always tell them:

ZAZEL: "Have pride in yourself. Don't assume something is impossible. Just ask. You will be amazed at what can happen."

(All clap two times.)

ALL: 2008.

CHRISTOPHER: I am determined to make it as an actor. I am dying to join Actors' Equity. I hear about a director named Ping Chong creating a show about people with disabilities. I have never heard of him, but it sounds cool. I don't need to worry if I am too disabled or not disabled enough. I can just be myself. I am invited to be in *Inside/Out*. And, because of this show, I finally get to join Equity!

(All clap two times.)

ALL: 2009.

MATTHEW: How do I negotiate the stares, the double takes, the giggles, the recoiling, the talking behind my back? Some days are better than others. In the end, I'm not the one with the problem. I've done nothing to make people afraid of me. Many years ago, I decided that I was not going to let anyone or anything stop me from living my life the way I want to. Not one day goes by without something positive happening to me. I know I'm fortunate because I know not everybody experiences that.

(All clap two times.)

ALL: 2009.

VIVIAN: Becoming legally blind is relatively new. It's still raw. Before now, I had hoped that my vision would improve. After twenty-one surgeries on my eyes, that hope is gone. I have reinvented myself many times during my lifetime:

ZAZEL: dancer,

MATTHEW: Peace Corps volunteer,

MONIQUE: mother,

BLAIR: student,

CHRISTOPHER: health care executive.

VIVIAN: Now, I am trying to reinvent myself as a legally blind person and member of the disability community.

(All clap two times.)

ALL: 2009.

JOSH: I am still trying to let my mother go. I am still trying to understand my relationship to my childhood, to illness and mortality, to community and intimacy. Finding a community of queer men and women and a community of artists helps. This is the great power of community, something my mother caught only fleeting glimpses of.

ALL: Change comes slowly.

(All clap two times.)

2009.

ZAZEL: My family in Montserrat looks at my sister, Cathy, like she's Jesus Christ because she's a judge. With me they say:

BLAIR: "Zazel, your foot not get betta?"

CHRISTOPHER: "Zazel, you still an artist?"

ZAZEL: Then they push me aside, but it doesn't bother me. If you want to leap across the stage and make that your life, why not? If you want to put ice cream in an ice-cream cone, why not? What's important is to be who you are and follow the direction you want to go in. That's what life should be about.

(All clap two times.)

ALL: 2009.

MONIQUE: I am an artist first. I do film. I draw and design and direct. I write lyrics and poetry, and I am trying to start my own live blues and hard rock band. I am an artist of all kinds. It has nothing to do with being deaf or speaking ASL. Art is a language that anyone can understand.

(All clap two times.)

ALL: 2009.

BLAIR: I feel comfortable with myself everywhere. You can run into ignorance and stereotyping anywhere, but we can change those assumptions through the media, through representation. We all have mixed abilities. We aren't the same but we aren't that different either.

(All clap ten times.

An uplifting choral song begins to play softly in the background. It continues through the finale.)

My name is Elizabeth Blair Wing. I was born on May 21, 1974, in Poughkeepsie, New York. My parents were happy I had all ten fingers and toes. It was spring.
　　Josh?

(She closes her script.)

JOSH: My name is Joshua Eric Hecht. I was born on June 5, 1978, at 3:45 P.M. in New York City. I weighed seven pounds, seven ounces. It was spring.
　　Vivian?

(He closes his script and stands.)

VIVIAN: My name is Vivian Cary Jenkins. I was born in Brooklyn, New York, at Beth-El Hospital on May 31, 1943, at 7:45 P.M. I weighed six pounds, four ounces. It was spring.
　　Zazel?

(She closes her script and stands.)

ZAZEL: My name is Zazel Chavah O'Garra. I was born on January 5, 1963, in Jamaica, Queens. I weighed seven pounds, eleven ounces. It was winter.
　　Monique?

(She closes her script and stands.)

MONIQUE: My name is Monique Bok Holt. The details of my birth are unknown. I arrived in the United States in 1970. It was autumn. Chris?

(She closes her script and stands.)

CHRISTOPHER: My name is Christopher Imbrosciano. I was born on July 27, 1984, in Edison, New Jersey. My parents were told there was a ninety-five percent chance that I would not live past my first birthday. I'm now twenty-four years old. It was summer. Matthew?

(He closes his script and stands.)

MATTHEW: My name is Matthew Seth Joffe. I was born on June 15, 1953, in New York City. My mother liked the name Matthew because it sounded musical to her. It was spring.

(He closes his script and stands.
Music up. The performers face the audience as the lights fade to blackout.)

END

Collaborator Interviews

An Oral History of an Oral History:
Voices of *Undesirable Elements*

Interviews by Victoria Abrash

PING CHONG

Creator, the *Undesirable Elements* series

VA: How did the *Undesirable Elements* series begin?

PC: *Undesirable Elements* was unlike anything I had ever done. I was as flabbergasted by it as anyone.

In the summer of 1992, I was teaching a ten-day course in stage design in Amsterdam. The students were international students from Bulgaria, Romania, Ireland, the United States, Holland, Israel. There was a woman of Shanghai ancestry who grew up in Sao Paulo, Brazil, married an American Jewish archeologist and moved to Israel—the perfect *Undesirable Elements* background.

We'd go out drinking, and when people had enough to drink, they'd revert to their own languages. We had this babble of languages flying around the bar. So that's how the idea for *Undesirable Elements* started. I thought, I wonder if I could make a show using multiple languages.

Later that fall, I was asked to do an installation at the New York City gallery Artists Space. I decided to do a piece about the rise of the religious right and intolerance in the United States. The result was *A Facility for the Channeling and Containment of Undesirable Elements*. It was an ambiguous installation and never named what were undesirable elements. The operative metaphor for the installation was a quarantine facility. The audience was quarantined on catwalks throughout the installation.

Then, Carlos Gutierrez-Solana, the executive director of Artists Space, asked me to make a performance piece for the installation. In an act of fate, I chose not to look for performers, just people who were fluent in English and also in a different native language. I didn't know where this was going. That first gathering of people in my tiny apartment included a Nicaraguan, a Lebanese-Venezuelan, a Japanese expatriate, a Ukrainian, a German, a Filipino and a Native American.

I asked them questions about food, proverbs. I was groping in the dark. As each person told me stories, it got my juices going. Once we got going, I realized that there were two places where they used their native languages: if they sang and in poetry. I wasn't interested in translation. I wanted the audience to hear the language. But the languages were the catalyst for what the show became, the starting point, not the end. The work is both an affirmation of difference and about the consequences of difference. Cause and effect.

How did you arrive at the structure of the Undesirable Elements works?

The pieces are organized in chronological order. Which brings us to the subject of time.

People tend to see my work as about otherness. Because I am an immigrant, otherness is in the work, and I've always been fascinated by difference and culture. But people miss that my work is also about time. The use of chronology has been in my work as early as *Humboldt's Current* in 1977. So organizing *Undesirable Elements* along a chronological structure was natural to me.

The first *Undesirable Elements* was different in some ways than the show is today. It was only forty minutes long. There weren't even music stands. But the template was there. Chronology was the structure of the show and it still is. The act of naming began the show and it always begins the show. In fact, the whole show is the act of naming, claiming one's identity. It's also very much about storytelling, the earliest, elemental form of theater.

How did an installation performance in New York end up being replicated all over the world?

We didn't publicize the first show. The press was not invited. The installation could only hold a tiny audience. It was so different from

PING CHONG

my previous work, I had no idea how it would be received and had no expectations.

But a festival director saw the show and asked if I would make a version of it in Cleveland. And Hiroshi Takahagi, the Japanese producer, also saw it at Artists Space and asked me to create a version in Tokyo. Between 1992 and 1995, I created five different productions in the *Undesirable Elements* series for different communities. *Undesirable Elements/Twin Cities* toured for over ten years on and off. And more and more communities of different types realized that the work spoke to and for them, and commissioned new pieces. And the productions sort of just grew.

How did the work evolve?

The early pieces were about language. But other differences came into the mix over time at the request of the commissioners.

Undesirable Elements/Twin Cities in 1994 was the first piece that was consciously about the place in which it was set. Up to that point, the piece had been a meditation on culture and living in America. The Twin Cities piece focused specifically on what it was to be an outsider living in the Minneapolis area.

The examination of place became more of a focus when we made the Tokyo production in 1995. Japan has very restrictive immigration laws, so the idea of a foreigner in Japan is quite different from the American context. We named this production *Gaijin*, Japanese slang for "foreigner," with a distinctly negative connotation.

When did the series begin to become more thematic?

In 2000, I created an all Asian production for NYU's Asian/Pacific/America Studies Program, which was called *Secret Histories*. The production was still geographically focused, but it was more specific than previous productions. The piece looked at what was similar and different among people of Asian and Pacific Island cultural backgrounds.

2001 was an important year for the series. The Spoleto Festival commissioned me to create a piece about the history of Charleston, South Carolina. We explored Native American history, patterns of immigration, race history there—and particularly the silence in the community about race history. I found it fascinating. I'd been to Charleston many times but had no idea that the street that I always crossed was a boundary that black residents were not historically allowed to cross.

167

The *Undesirable Elements/Atlanta* production in 2001 was the first to have a youth focus. In 2002, I was asked to make *Children of War*, which focused on children who had survived wars in their home countries and now lived in the Washington, D.C., area. It was very powerful. And to celebrate the tenth anniversary of *Undesirable Elements*, we brought together people from many different productions to make *UE 92/02*, and my managing director, Bruce Allardice, came up with the idea that I should be in it. That brought the project full circle in a sense.

How have you worked with other collaborators on these pieces?

We always partnered with community organizations because we were making productions in different places, so the idea of collaboration was built into the structure of the piece. So it seemed natural to have creative collaborators as the project developed.

Michael Rohd was one of my first collaborators in creating an *Undesirable Elements* piece. He worked with me on *Undesirable Elements/Chicago* in 1999 and grew to be a co-writer, working on *Undesirable Elements/Hanover* and *Undesirable Elements/Berlin*. I also collaborated with Michael on my interdisciplinary plays, *Blind Ness* and *Truth & Beauty*, both of which were documentary-based works, outside the *Undesirable Elements* series.

Talvin Wilks was the dramaturg on the 1995 *Undesirable Elements/Seattle* production at the Group Theatre and has now co-written and directed several works in the series. He worked on *Secret Histories: Charleston* and *Undesirable Elements/Atlanta* in 2001, and many others. We asked him to interview me and script the 2002 anniversary production *UE 92/02*.

The anniversary show included another alumnus of the 1995 Seattle production, Iranian-American, Leyla Modirzadeh. She collaborated with me several times and, in 2008, made her own *Undesirable Elements* piece, *Secret Histories: Oxford*, in Oxford, Mississippi.

Sara Zatz has been a close collaborator and has worked with me at Ping Chong + Company for many years. She started in 2000 as the production manager for *Secret Histories*. In 2004, she started writing with me for *Secret Histories: Seattle Youth*, the production we made for the Seattle Repertory Theatre, and then we split the writing on the 2005 production on Native American identity, *Native Voices— Secret History*. In 2007, she scripted the *Undesirable Elements/Asian America* production in New York on her own, and I came in to give my input later. We wrote the script for *Inside/Out . . . voices from the disability community* production together in 2008, and Sara independently wrote and directed *Secret Survivors*, with adult survivors of childhood sexual abuse. Sara now oversees all projects in development.

Jesca Prudencio, who joined the Ping Chong + Company staff in 2008, is my newest collaborator. She was my assistant director on *Secret History: The Philadelphia Story*, our *Undesirable Elements* in Philly with urban and suburban youth, and she and Sara developed Secret Histories, the *Undesirable Elements* arts-in-education program in the New York City public schools, which began in 2008. Jesca now oversees the education program and is our lead teaching artist.

How do you make the show work in such different contexts?

The show is very adaptable. It can be done in the round, proscenium-style, in a theater or a community center. It can be incredibly low-tech or with lots of production elements. It's very versatile in that way. It was even done in a beauty parlor once.

I'm a great admirer of the Japanese filmmaker Ozu, who insisted on severe limitations on his film work. In his mature work, he never moved the camera. *Undesirable Elements* is my Ozu.

How has *Undesirable Elements* changed over time?

If you look at the first script, my hand is on it more than the individuals' hands. Because I didn't know what it was yet. As time goes by, I find my role to be more about giving voice to others whose voices are not heard in our community.

But it's remarkable how much from that very first production has held. The floor is usually covered in rock salt, which is a carryover from the original production. The visual of a full moon and a half moon; the half moon shape of the seating. The audience is the other half of that moon. The full moon image functions in many ways. It's a metaphor for what we aspire to: wholeness.

Some productions have added installation elements. The 1995 *Undesirable Elements/Seattle* production had a vitrine of cast members' mementos at the front of the stage. *Delta Rising*, the 2008 production about people from the Mississippi Delta living in New York, used original projection and family photographs, as did *Tales from the Salt City*. The *Undesirable Elements/Rotterdam*, production in the Netherlands, in 1997, included an installation of passports and photos.

I love all of the *Undesirable Elements*, but I miss the "cultural" ones if we don't do them for a while, because of my fascination with the construct of culture. For those, we always have a pot-luck meal where everyone brings their traditional food.

How has Undesirable Elements had an impact?

I think that it's helped change people's consciousness. At a talk-back after a performance of *Secret Histories: Charleston*, a woman who came out as gay during the show talked to a man who said, "I don't like gay people, but now, after hearing your story, I have to think about that." A boy who saw the *Undesirable Elements/Cleveland* production when it toured to Kent State University in Ohio turned up years later working at the Seattle Rep. He said, "That show changed my view of the world." *Native Voices*, in Lawrence, Kansas, was in a seven-hundred-seat theater and people still responded to it personally.

It's real people up there. That's the power of it. It's not actors, it's real people telling their own stories. And they always receive standing ovations.

TALVIN WILKS
Collaborator

VA: How did you get involved in *Undesirable Elements?*

TW: I first encountered *Undesirable Elements* in the fall of 1994 when I went to work at the Group Theatre in Seattle as a writer-in-residence and literary manager. *Undesirable Elements/Seattle* premiered in Seattle in the spring of 1995. Ping had a TCG artist residency at the Group and was developing an original play, but the Group Theatre decided to commission an *Undesirable Elements* piece instead of producing that work.

I was excited to be working with Ping. I admired his work, but I didn't know him at that time. I hadn't seen *Undesirable Elements* in New York, and I didn't know anything about it, but it quickly became clear that I would inherit the role of writer and dramaturg. I just happened to be in the right place at the right time.

The *Undesirable Elements* process and the idea of Ping working with a collaborative artist were evolving at the time. Ping had worked with a dramaturg and liked the idea of having someone to bounce ideas off of. He requested someone to track the scripts and be a partner with him in notating the interviews and generating language from the interviews for the show.

We also created a museum case of artifacts from people's lives that reflected their cultures. It was a curatorial job that was part of the dramaturgical collaboration. I had never done anything like that before, but it was a wonderful collaboration.

Over the years I've learned the style of the Ping Chong interview technique. The *Undesirable Elements* form has evolved as well, regarding the information Ping is interested in. When I look back at that Seattle script, it was so simple. The entries are so short. We have eight people telling their stories, and the show was still under ninety minutes. The entries now are more subtle, more intertwined. The form has evolved in a wonderful way. It's more provocative and evocative now.

How did you come to collaborate with Ping after that first production?

Ping Chong + Company approached me in 2001 to work on *Secret Histories: Charleston*, and that was the next time I got involved. Very specifically, they got in touch with me because they knew the piece would involve race and a Southern background, a history and perspective that I do have through my grandparents. I think Ping wanted me to help navigate the complexities of race in the South and issues of black and white. He has his own perspective on race in America. That was the piece when I feel we really were a duo, a creative team. Before that, I was dramaturgical support.

The Charleston piece was an interesting one because it was a transition. Called *Secret Histories*, it was more a history of a place than the previous productions had been. It told the cultural history of Charleston. It was produced under the umbrella of a project called *Evoking History*, which was a companion to the Spoleto Festival that year. A lot of artists came in for the project to read the cultural landscape of Charleston, especially along the lines of race and community.

It worked incredibly well. The interesting thing about this notion of *Secret Histories* as opposed to *Undesirable Elements* is that it wasn't so much about the unfamiliar. The form served the history of that place incredibly well. There was a history of shared-ness and community beyond the black/white view that is often referred to. A white man in the audience got up at the end and said to one of the African-American performers, "I think you're my cousin." He recognized something in her story, and they found out that they were cousins.

It was fascinating to research the history of Charleston and evoke it. Black people were still segregated in that community, and people were not sharing their stories as a rule. In some way, we were freed by our show to discover bridges. We were involved in a lot of community events and the *Evoking History* project situated our piece in the middle of a larger conversation. It worked. *Secret Histories* was a very successful community-articulation and -sharing.

The cast included a woman from Eritrea and an Ojibwe woman who had rediscovered her culture. The others were from the area: a Gullah woman from the islands and a poor white woman, who was a lesbian, and came out through this piece. The participants were not defined by being from other cultures but from their connection to Charleston's culture. We continued to explore and discover that more.

For the 2008 production of *Delta Rising*, about people from the Mississippi Delta living in New York, we shifted the framework. It was completely different again for the 2009 *Women of the Hill* in Pittsburgh. That cast was all African-American women from one neighborhood. Issues within a particular community, like class and skin color, still worked in that *Undesirable Elements* framework of otherness. Also in 2001, I collaborated on *Undesirable Elements/ Atlanta*, one of the first all-youth projects.

We also experimented with making a conglomerate of different pieces for Ping's thirtieth anniversary, which was also the tenth anniversary of *Undesirable Elements*. We chose people from different places and productions to create a new show: *UE 92/02*. This was also the first production of *Undesirable Elements* that Ping performed in, so I interviewed him and placed his story in this group. The success of that production led us to tour it internationally, to Lille, France, and the RomaEuropa Festival in Italy.

Tell us about *Women of the Hill*.

The production of *Women of the Hill* in Pittsburgh was my idea. I commissioned this piece for the August Wilson Center to be the community performance piece of a larger project called *The Aunt Esther Cycle*, which brought together a number of plays by August Wilson connected by the recurring character of Aunt Esther. I wanted to explore the diversity in what seems like a homogenous community and to tell a collective history of a place. The piece tells the history of the Hill District of Pittsburgh, where almost all of August Wilson's plays are set, through the voices of women who live there. I wanted women to help contextualize the history of *The Aunt Esther Cycle*. There were six black women with a diversity of class, an age range of thirties to seventies, diversity of education. Color-consciousness is a big story within this group of women. They cover a broad range, even though they are all African American. All the ideas that *Undesirable Elements* brings forth hold true within this community even though it might look homogenous.

It's interesting for the future trajectory of *Undesirable Elements* to see that it can attach to another curatorial lens and stay intact. When people are looking at the project, there's a track record of how it can shift and morph, yet stay intact and effective. The interview process remains the same, the structure remains the same: they can accommodate different curatorial ideas and the piece retains its integrity.

What about *Delta Rising*?

Ping was in for the first interviews. I really ran rehearsals and introduced a new visual element: video projections of personal artifacts. This is another way our collaboration has evolved. I'm able to bring new aesthetics, understanding the work and how it evolves.

Delta Rising had unusual needs. It was about people from the Delta living in New York, but they were of different cultural lineages: the Delta Chinese, the strong Jewish traditions. It was a piece about the Delta and what they carried with them from the Delta, even though they find themselves somewhere else. I wanted a shift to include more cultural information. We used blues music. The effect of the museum artifacts from my first *Undesirable Elements* in Seattle, which I was always enamored with, was created now with video. People brought in newspaper clippings, photos, old maps, artifacts, and we worked with projection designer Maya Ciarrocchi to make a video of them. It was really beautiful

Ping himself began to change the rules behind *Undesirable Elements*. I find myself preserving rules that he's let go of. Each event has allowed the possibility of new ideas that impact the next event.

It's because of the strength of the structure that you can imagine new ways of telling stories and finding cultural resonance. You never quite know with each group if you'll have a dancer, a singer. Will poems work? Will songs? In the process, you're looking for humor, pathos, triumph. *Delta Rising* had a lot of good jokes in it. *Women of the Hill* had poetry, some original, some traditional. For me, even within the structure of *Undesirable Elements*, the pieces have always been incredibly creative and original.

You helped found the *Undesirable Elements* Training Institute?

The company came up with the idea of starting a summer training program, as a way to train other people in the process of developing work using the *Undesirable Elements* process. They asked me to help develop a curriculum and a plan. In doing so, we found ourselves for the first time really thinking about defining a methodology and defining what we do in creating an *Undesirable Elements* piece.

We had to analyze the work we had been doing for years. How do you break this down into the fundamental components? What is the pedagogy behind the process? How can one effectively learn this methodology?

The first step was a series of conversations with Ping, Sara [Zatz], Jesca [Prudencio] and Bruce [Allardice], the Ping Chong staff, to really pinpoint what we thought the process was. Once we had articulated that, I started to build a curriculum around those components.

We decided that the workshop should be built around people developing their own oral history pieces inspired by the *Undesirable Elements* methodology. We created a fairly traditional one-week-residence process to teach this methodology to community members, artists, activists and educators who were really interested in oral history, art and social justice.

For our pilot project, we were interested in a situation in which students could get credit; we were concerned about diversity; we wanted to be intergenerational; and we wanted to be selective, not just an open first-come-first-served process. Sara and I created an application process with a questionnaire about their background, and their interest in the project and in art and social justice. We decided that the Ko Festival at Amherst College in Massachusetts would be the best fit to host the inaugural workshop, since I had a relationship with the festival and its director Sabrina Hamilton, and knew the location and setup, and Ping had been an early artist-in-residence at the Ko Festival.

We got more than forty inquiries from all over the world for the ten to fifteen places we could accommodate in the pilot Institute. We reached out through list-serves, organizations and publications. We weren't just looking for theater folks. We whittled it down to a final group of fifteen wonderful participants from Thailand, Hawaii, all throughout the United States. This was great for the Ko Festival, since usually their residencies are local, and great for the workshop. We had local and national representation, a very diverse group in background, age, gender, in all ways.

Sara and I co-facilitated the week-long Institute. A large part of the process was training how to conduct, edit and animate interviews. We also embedded two master classes with Ping during the week, around his larger aesthetic, his movement vocabulary and visual aesthetic. There was also an art and social justice aspect to the work. Participants were also able to bring their own practices into the mix and incorporate their own interests and backgrounds into the process.

Each session had a lesson and a practicum component. We drew on the curriculum from the *Undesirable Elements* education program in the schools as well: exercises with story circle, sense of memoir—approaches that work well with large groups and get people thinking about memoir. The Institute participants then learned techniques and experimented with their own entries, creating their own stories, interviewing each other, crafting those pieces into what we call the "structured sound-bites" of the *Undesirable Elements* script. Work began with two team partners working together, then continued in groups. At the end of the Institute process, five groups each presented a five- to ten-minute complete piece.

Creating the Institute curriculum really strengthened our understanding of what it is that we do and how we do it. That was very exciting. It reaffirmed Ping's belief that the process is trainable and flexible. We now have a curricula and a training manual about how one can think about crafting an *Undesirable Elements* project, what are the cultural components we look for, how we build a story. The Training Institute is now one of the clear anchors of the *Undesirable Elements* work. It roots *Undesirable Elements* as a practice that can be recognized and taught in addition to how it continues to evolve in the company's community collaborations.

Seeing the results, what the participants created, how they took the form and found their own way into the form, was inspiring to us, and gave us new ways of thinking about *Undesirable Elements*, which will show up in the work moving forward.

What can you tell us about the interview process?

There are so many things that come out in the interview process. How open are they? Do they have a unique story to tell? A unique character? Personality? Sometimes it's a great story, but not a great storyteller. Those are the most painful. Sometimes they're like therapy sessions. For many of them it's the first time they've told the story or the first time in a very long time and even they are surprised by how emotional they are.

The interview process is everything for me. Having learned so well from Ping, in process, you're writing entries even as you do the interview. You can already begin to transform the interview into the piece as you work. You can hear it. That comes from experience.

Ping guides the interviews. He jots down specific things. When we were doing interviews for *Women of the Hill*, there was a throughline about generational music. He'll say, "Follow that line," "Pick up on this." Sara Zatz has become much more instrumental as an editor. Ping is more of an auteur, thinking of the arc and structure, the sound of things and the rhythm of things. On some shows, Ping does everything. In partnership, he can relinquish elements, which allows him to do more. As a team, we are all working toward the best script of those collective stories. However the collaborations work, and they vary, the team can deliver a strong *Undesirable Elements* project. The impact has always been very successful and greatly appreciated by every community where we've been.

There are often talk-backs after performances or social occasions to communicate with the audience. The appreciation of the community for the richness they discover is amazing. There's a new appreciation of the diversity of the people in their midst. "Oh my god, I didn't even know this existed!" It really helps a community to understand how people got there and the risks they took. It changes the conversation.

Undesirable Elements provides a fuller human story that you never would have had access to otherwise. The way that multiple voices are heard breaks through prejudices. That's what I love so much about this piece, its ability to change the conversation. I've seen it every time in every place we've done the show.

SARA ZATZ

Associate Director, Ping Chong + Company / Project Director of the *Undesirable Elements* series

VA: How did you first come to *Undesirable Elements*?

SZ: The first *Undesirable Elements* that I encountered was the 2000 production of *Secret History* at the Ohio Theatre in New York. I had interned at Ping Chong + Company and I was hired as production supervisor for the piece. I came in for three weeks and coordinated the production side of it.

Hearing Tania Salmen's story of growing up in war-torn Beirut was the part that stood out for me: the mix of obvious tragic elements and the pure joy of her dance. What I remember taking away from that production of *Secret History* was the balance of social justice and "real" theater. This piece walked the line of political engagement and entertainment. It struck the perfect balance, making a point but not pointing a finger at the audience.

In 2002, I was hired full-time to coordinate the *Undesirable Elements* project. Ping Chong + Company had received a Ford Foundation grant to expand *Undesirable Elements*. The grant came from the Human Rights division, not the theater division. After ten years of one thing leading to another, the project was growing and the company needed more support. This was the moment to grow it and formalize it more. I became full-time staff in July, leading up to the *Undesirable Elements/Hanover* production at Dartmouth College in August. *UE 92/02*, the tenth anniversary production, was performed in New York that October. The interview process was beginning for *Children of War* in Washington, D.C., and *Undesirable Elements/ Berlin* with the House of World Cultures was in development.

Children of War was the first *Undesirable Elements* project I was involved with from the beginning. It was also the first project that I worked with Ping on the interviews. For *Children of War* we had a lot of support from the Center for Multicultural Services. Because the performers were young, they prescreened and selected people for us to meet.

The single most powerful part of *Undesirable Elements* for me continues to be meeting the people from every experience, from all over the world and having the privilege to hear their stories. There are so many questions you'd like to ask people who are different from you, and you can, you have to, for *Undesirable Elements*. "When have you been treated like an outsider?" "What was it like when you walked into the store and they followed you?" You just can't ask these questions at a cocktail party. Nowadays a simple question can seem coded and it can be challenging to even ask, "Where are you from?" In *Undesirable Elements* you really discover people's stories.

In the rehearsal and interview, there's an intimate exchange. Hopefully, we're taking the experience of the interview and passing it on to the audience shaped and edited. There's definitely intimacy, and I know the audience feels privileged to hear these stories.

Ping and I became very good interview partners. We're different ages, ethnicities, genders, family backgrounds, so I might relate to things a little differently than he does, which is good for the project. Then in 2004, in Seattle for *Secret Histories: Seattle Youth* at the Seattle Repertory Theatre, Ping said, "Do you want to write?" From 2004–2007, we began splitting the writing half and half. There were always multiple projects going on, and Ping couldn't do it all, and we worked together very well. The first project on which I took the lead was, ironically, *Undesirable Elements/Asian America* in 2007. I did the primary writing and directing on that, though Ping was also involved and responded to the script and gave plenty of input.

I have to give Ping as an artist an incredible amount of credit because he came to me and said, "Do you want to take this on?" Any time I reached a certain level, he'd help me move on and made sure that I had the support I needed and that I got credit. He does that for all of his collaborators.

I often say that *Undesirable Elements* is like a sonnet, it has finite rules, but within those rules you have a lot of freedom. I model my work on Ping's. If we split the interviews half and half, people can't usually tell the difference. If there's a performer who I relate to more, I try to do that script session. We pick the people we can do the best by their story. We always work on the editing together, whatever seams might show are polished to make a unified piece.

In the beginning, we both try to overwrite, so we can polish and cut and scale back. Sometimes one of us wants to cut something and the other says it's really important. At some point, one or the other says, "You were so right." It's effective to have multiple writers to get some perspective on things. It's easier for me to edit Ping's work and for him to edit mine.

How has the process of creating *Undesirable Elements* changed?

Ping had already been creating *Undesirable Elements* texts for about ten years when I came in, but he'd been doing it with little help. He had all the interview questions in his head. As more collaborators came into the process, we needed a system. I took the interview process I had observed with Ping and formalized it. There were certain questions Ping always asked: "Where were you born?" "How did your parents meet?" Cultural holidays. He always asked people for six names from their culture or a poem or a song. I generated a questionnaire which organized the process. It has been an effective system. We can ask our partners to have participants complete the form when we first start. Then I created a participants' requirement list based on the questions that our partners on the projects always ask me. So we have a good packet of information for partners from the start.

How do the producing partnerships work?

The ideal situation for creating an *Undesirable Elements* work is a partnership between Ping Chong + Company, a local arts partner, and a community-based or social service organization with close ties to the population represented in the piece. Ping Chong + Company has self-produced in New York. In those cases, we are the social service organization, the local organization and the arts organization all in one.

The partner organization does the recruiting for the performance. It lines up twenty people or so for us to meet at first, according to our guidelines and their goals. *Undesirable Elements* is always community-specific, with new people in every city. We have done some "all-star" productions, bringing in people from different cities, and some performers have been in more than one production, if their story and background are appropriate.

The most common way for *Undesirable Elements* pieces to happen has been that someone saw a production and said, "Boy, would I love to do this in my community." We've been lucky that it's been self-propelled. People from all kinds of different communities have found us. But there are many organizations and communities out there that could benefit from *Undesirable Elements*, but might not know about it and would like to. That's one of the reasons that this book is important.

There are many different options for groups interested in bringing the *Undesirable Elements* experience to their communities: They could commission a full production from Ping Chong + Company. They could send someone to train with us to create a piece. Or they could do a mini-residency. At the end of the day, it's always been Ping Chong's *Undesirable Elements*, and it always will be, but what's most important is the history of the work and the impact it has. The *Undesirable Elements* projects can be done in any community. Many of the productions have been commissioned by organizations that are not theaters. The Chicago YMCA, Atlanta Big Brothers and Big Sisters; *Children of War* was commissioned by a social service organization.

One of the brilliant things about the structure Ping developed is that it's completely flexible. It looks best under great lighting with projections and a thousand pounds of rock salt covering the floor, as it was originally conceived, but, in the end, it's about the stories and it can be done with nothing but chairs in a community center and be powerful.

What is the range of communities you've worked with on this project?

Since I started on the *Undesirable Elements* project, we've done *Children of War*, about young refugees from war; *Native Voices–Secret History*, which was all Native American participants (And I have to say that was a really powerful project for me, to re-learn American history. Hearing American history from the Native perspective; it's not how I learned it, and I got to do a lot of research. It was eye-opening.); an Asian-American production, *Undesirable Elements/Asian America*;

three pieces that focused on disability, including *Inside/Out, Invisible Voices* and *Undesirable Elements/Albuquerque*; a refugee piece, *Secret History: Journeys Abroad, Journeys Within*; two Mississippi pieces, *Delta Rising* and *Secret Histories/Oxford*; *Women of the Hill*, with African-American women in Pittsburgh; *Tales from the Salt City*, with members of the Syracuse community from all backgrounds; another Syracuse production, *Cry for Peace*, with refugees from the ongoing conflicts in the Congo; and *Secret Survivors*, with adults who survived child sexual abuse. And those are just some of them, so it's a pretty incredible range! We have also started a Training Institute, which was first held in 2011 at Amherst College as part of the Ko Festival, and a program in the New York City public schools.

What is the casting process like?

When you are doing a piece with a social theme, you want to be sure that you have a range of participants. You don't want all the participants to be the same age, gender, class or to have grown up in the same circumstances. Unless that's the theme.

The powerful thing about *Undesirable Elements*, for the past twenty years, is that it's real people telling their own stories. When a performer cries on opening night remembering his father, it's real and raw, not acting. The structure accommodates for non-actors in a way that's great. They have scripts so they don't have to memorize. They are presented as real people so the audience is open and generous in a way they might not be with actors. The human frailty of performance is such that if someone slips, the audience accepts it in a way they might not with actors. That the performers are real people telling their own stories, not actors, is built into the piece in a way that really works.

The audience response is always amazing. There are three types of audience members: One, people who are somehow connected, and there's so much power in seeing the stories that they can relate to onstage, often in places they never see people like themselves. Second is the more typical audience member for whom this is an unusual theater experience. Third is the person who has come to the theater for a theater experience. I'm always pleased when a theater snob responds to *Undesirable Elements*. And they do.

You can tell these stories in a compelling way that is not narrative but is theatrical. It's hard to explain. "You mean it's not a play?" But the show is always very moving. At the end of the day, that's your measure; how the audience responds. It's always very powerful.

It works for regular theatergoers, but it also gets non-mainstream theater audiences to come to the theater. Something different is happening onstage and also in the audience. You go to so much theater and see a sea of white faces. You go to *Undesirable Elements* and see the most diverse audiences I've ever seen.

Every *Undesirable Elements* project is always deeply grounded in Ping Chong's work and vision. Ping has created a unique method of creating oral history theater works that has proven to be remarkably strong, effective and adaptable. It works for so many themes and issues and communities, and we've shown that it is an approach that can be learned and developed by carefully trained artists. I'm very, very privileged to do this work.

TIMOTHY BOND

Commissioner and Producing Partner, The Group Theatre,
Undesirable Elements/Seattle; Syracuse Stage, *Tales from the
Salt City* and *Cry for Peace: Voices from the Congo*

TB: When I first met Ping, he described the first *Undesirable Elements* project, which he had just worked on, how it started with an installation, and he added people to it, and developed the idea of sharing the stories of people who had been seen as undesirable. And I really related to that.

I had trained at the Group Theatre in Seattle, which was one of the nation's first multicultural theaters, then called "multiethnic." And being a person who's tricultural myself—Native American, African American and European American—I am acutely aware of a dysphoria that results from never fully feeling understood or accepted into certain communities. So the notion of "undesirable elements" struck a real personal chord for me.

And as an artist who had been working on and directing and producing plays for years dealing with the concept of otherness, I found in Ping Chong a master artist who was really dealing with this on a master scale. So I was really interested in having him come to make a piece with us, exploring the diverse voices of people from the Seattle community.

Decades later, when I came to Syracuse, I felt instantly what a diverse mélange of people were living here, but they didn't feel that they had a platform to find their voices on the stage. And in my very first season at Syracuse Stage, I wanted to bring Ping out to explore the immigrant voices that had been such a part of the history of Syracuse, to show their struggles and their triumphs, and to, ultimately, show that Syracuse had found a way to integrate those voices into its identity. I wanted to see how Ping could address that.

It was the first idea I had when I got the job. I think I called Bruce [Allardice, managing director, Ping Chong + Company] before I even got the job. I said, "I don't know if this is going to happen but I might be the artistic director of a theater again, and if I am you'll hear from me." It was so clear that I needed to do this here.

Native Americans had to be included (the people who were here before the European immigrants arrived). We are always looking at what has been preserved and what has been lost here in Syracuse, so we have to start from the beginning. I find so few artists who understand that root approach. Because of my Native American ancestry, it's important to me that we don't skip that beginning.

One of the things I've learned from Ping through the years is looking for connections across ethnic, racial and cultural lines. Those connections allow anyone to take a journey back through their own family ancestral experience, even if their ancestry is not one of those represented onstage. Those journeys that everyone has taken in our families are similar, and those similarities bond us. The way Ping creates *Undesirable Elements* is unique in its ability to show us that.

That's what all great theater does. Ultimately it's about our humanity. It overcomes all the politics and religion and other divisive issues and biases that separate us.

In *Undesirable Elements*, people voice each other's stories and enter into each other's stories in a way that is seamless and that is the truth. We are more alike than we are different. And what's different about us is to be celebrated, not feared. That comes through so strongly and without having to state it. That's one of the real powers of the form that Ping has created.

How was the process of working with Ping Chong?

Ping is one of the greatest collaborators on the planet. That's all there is to it. He is a singular artist with a singular vision but he really takes in what's around him. Ping is amazing. He comes into a new community and susses it out very quickly. He's a people person, and he quickly feels a vibe and adapts himself to that. Sara [Zatz, project director, *Undesirable Elements*] is terrific, too, and having them work together was terrific.

What was the impact of Undesirable Elements on your audiences?

It was a pretty spot-on sell for my audience in Seattle. The Group Theatre audience was energized and prepared and ready to take that journey. They embraced the piece wholeheartedly. It was everything I'd hoped. You might say it was preaching to the choir, but people came to our theater who had never come before. It expanded our mission and made what we'd been talking about and doing for years even broader and clearer. It wasn't just about American "minorities," a term I don't use, but which others always applied to us. *Undesirable Elements* was an authentic global inclusion of people from any number of backgrounds that added up to the human story. It was really one of the most satisfying experiences for me as artistic director of the Group.

When I arrived at Syracuse Stage I wanted to do the same thing. I knew that prior to my coming here, the theater had not embraced voices from our own community so much. Now we are expanding our vision of what we mean when we say we are serving our community. I wanted it to be very clear, which it is in *Undesirable Elements*, when we invite our broader community to our audience and our stage.

When *Tales from the Salt City* opened, I got the most amazing responses: "I've been coming to this theater for three decades and this is the most amazing piece of theater I've ever seen." "It's life-changing. I'm so glad I saw it. I have a totally different view of people walking down the street now. People whose lives I never even thought about." People would make these comments, often in tears. "How did he do that?" It was a step on our journey to audience inclusion.

Ping created a unique Seattle *Undesirable Elements* and a unique Syracuse one. The productions held a mirror up to the community. That's what great art is. Ping does it totally from a place of curiosity and interest in the other, and he lives that. Wherever he goes, he's going to find out what the cultures and clashes are and bring them to light. What he does is extraordinary.

TIMOTHY BOND is the Producing Artistic Director of Syracuse Stage and the Syracuse University Department of Drama. He has more than twenty years experience in leading regional theaters throughout the country, including five years as Artistic Director of the Seattle Group Theatre, where he commissioned *Undesirable Elements/Seattle* in 1995.

FARINAZ AMIRSEHI

Performer, *Children of War*

VA: How did you first encounter *Undesirable Elements*?

FA: At the time, I was working as a therapist at the Center for Multi-cultural Human Services. Frankly I had no idea that this project was happening. I was fully involved with working with providing mental health services for survivors of politically motivated torture under a UN grant.

Our director, Dr. Dennis Hunt, told me about this project. He knew about my background as a political prisoner in my homeland, Iran, and he said it would be good to have a therapist involved who also has experience in this area. Ping interviewed me and I was the last addition to the cast.

I was excited when I heard this. It was really interesting, because I had never done such a thing and never even heard of such a thing. It gave a whole different perspective on trauma. And because the focus was on children, it made the experience more tangible for people. It was a very good medium to raise awareness of trauma, and that's invaluable—you can't put any price on that.

How did you feel about the children in the show telling their stories of surviving war?

Here's the deal. These were kids. It's very different if an adult is telling his or her story. An adult, developmentally it's expected that they have reached a point of ego-strength to be able to handle it. Chances are they have been through therapy so they have the foundations for modulating emotions and stress that may be induced by retelling their story. But these are kids.

Was it therapeutic for the kids? Absolutely. Because people have no idea what trauma can mean for a child and how it can affect a child. They found an audience who cared and who was willing to listen and validate what they went through, their feelings and experiences.

It was a difficult project because they were kids. Each one of them went through the public school system, and for the most part they were outcasts there. Nobody believed them there. Any problems they had academically or behaviorally they were labeled not good kids. But they were bearing a heavy burden. For the kids it was a validation of their story. Was it therapeutic for them? Absolutely. Did they need therapy afterward? Personally I think so.

Was it painful to share your story of being tortured as a political prisoner?

I'm an adult and I have done a ton of work on me. Was it painful? No. It wasn't painful at all. I had always been very open about my experiences. I had always been comfortable about my experiences. I had my moments when I had to swallow up my tears. But it wasn't painful for me. When I came to the States I was approached by several well-known people in the publishing field who wanted me to write a book about my experiences. I turned them down. I never was comfortable with the glorification of trauma. Because this is to me Hollywood stuff. People who go through trauma are real people with real experiences on all levels. They are not perfect. They are not the big hero who is the good guy who ends up killing the bad guy. And there's no glory in suffering. We're real people. We have our weaknesses, our down points, our flaws. I didn't want to contribute to anything like that. There have been many books on the conditions in Iran's prisons. How many times do you want to digest torture? What would you gain by that? The end result would be more of the victimization of the person who has gone through that: "Poor him or poor her, feel sorry for her," versus empowerment. Empowerment is seeing them as who they really are and seeing the power in that.

When this project came along I thought, This is it, it's about real people. I didn't want to write a book, because I didn't like the focus. But this project went along with my belief system, giving me the chance to be part of something very real, versus a glorified sob story.

It wasn't so much my story in particular, it was the interweaving of all the stories. I was the only adult, and it was a very good contrast with these children. The combination of the six stories provided that. Had any of us been doing this solo, I don't think it would have had the impact. It was seeing trauma through six different lenses. Six different parts of the world. Six different experiences. Some included war, some included domestic trauma. There was a variety of trauma.

There are a lot of books about someone's personal, one-and-only experience, and it's all good; but I don't think those books have the power that this project has.

Ping, Sara and Courtney, the stage manager, were so, so supportive. I remember there was a part in my script where I was talking about my mom, and it was only a few sentences, but I was choking up in tears the first few times I read it, and they stopped. They stopped the whole thing so I could recover. It was great. I was the first one to do that; after that the kids saw it was okay to emote. You have this support. It was not just "read your line and look good"; they cared about you. We were all supportive of each other. During the show, Yarvin was the most emotional. When she had her part, everyone sent supportive vibes to her. We were all concerned. We would wait and give the other person time. We were all present.

This is what I mean about being organic, it was real. There wasn't any acting. People were being themselves. All of us. That was a huge element in making it a success and believable.

I was surprised by the audience response. I've always been open about my experience. I went to school here, and whenever anything came up and I would mention my experience, it was like, "Stay away from here." Now people were coming up to us. It was very different.

Granted not everybody would go to such a show. But the number of people showing up was a surprise. Fairfax County Virginia's public television made a half-hour excerpt of the show and ran it every night for two years. I would go to Safeway and someone would say, "I saw you on TV last night." That's huge. That's how good the show was. It won a place on a daily basis on TV.

I don't know how Ping did it, but he nailed it. He met me, he had specific questions, and a timeline, and I filled in a questionnaire. I don't know how he was able to pick the critical parts of all that information and so beautifully weave it in to other people's stories. Some of the kids had some information that they weren't comfortable talking about. It would have been great if it had been shared, but Ping was great and understanding and conscientious not to push it. He went with the comfort level of the cast. I don't know how he did it. I'm in awe of his talents.

He went through numerous edits of the script based on not only what was good for this show, but based on each individual's comfort level. It was a long process, continually in progress. It kept changing, which was great. That's what made everyone comfortable. Their opinions were important. And they were taken into consideration.

I think that this is what sets him apart from many of his peers. To a lot of people, the script is the script and if there are any changes it's to accommodate the end result of the play or the movie, not to accommodate the individual. Ping did it differently and that's what makes him Ping.

For me, though I am an adult, there were many people who I had worked with who had no idea about this part of my life. Finally, there was the gratification that I was able to contribute something meaningful because of this experience. I was able to give the kids a lot of hope; the project gave them motivation, inspiration, to continue to live and be and do the best they can do, to know they're not tainted people; they can achieve.

Children of War was a gift, a privilege, an honor for every single one of us. I speak especially for myself.

Farinaz Amirsehi is a licensed professional counselor, a nationally certified counselor and a registered nurse. She has extensive experienced with severely traumatized populations and has provided training for professionals of different disciplines on the impact of trauma on body, mind and spirit.

FRANCES KAO

Commissioner and Producing Partner, Seattle Repertory
Theatre, *Secret Histories: Seattle Youth*

VA: When did you first encounter *Undesirable Elements*?

FK: Here at the Seattle Rep we've had a long-term artistic association
with Ping Chong. He was here with *Obon: Tales of Rain and Moon-
light*, and talked about the ten-year anniversary of *Undesirable Elements* and the production of *UE 92/02*, which was taking place in
New York City. I was lucky enough to have family on the east coast
at the time of the ten-year anniversary production at La Mama. That
was the first time that I saw an *Undesirable Elements* piece.

That production was the first one Ping was in. I was very moved
by it. I was split as I watched it. I was swept away by the emotional
roller coaster of the lives I was seeing. And the other part of me was
thinking, This could be done for my students at the Seattle Rep.
I came back and told Andrea Allen, director of education at Seattle
Rep, falling all over myself, "We have to do it! We have to do it!"

We had worked in so many high schools in Seattle through our
education partnerships. We envisioned an *Undesirable Elements*
with Seattle high school students. We went to our artistic director
at the time, Sharon Ott, and she, of course, had a good relationship
with Ping. Our managing director, Ben Moore, spoke with Bruce

[Allardice], Ping's managing director. And we commissioned *Secret Histories: Seattle Youth.*

How did *Secret Histories: Seattle Youth* take shape?

Ping came out with Sara Zatz [project director, *Undesirable Elements*]. Ping, Sara, Braden Abraham, now our associate artistic director, then literary manager, and myself, worked with the *Seattle Youth* participants to create the piece.

We focused on five stories. For three of those five storytellers, English was not their native language. In Abdi-Karim's case it might have been his fifth or sixth language. Ping put me into the show along with another student to narrate some of the show in order to alleviate some of the pressure on the non-native English speakers. Ping is a great artist and this allowed him to play with the language. One of our students, Pathiel, a survivor of the conflict in Sudan, had a lovely conversation with his mother, and Ping made it a dialogue with me. It was a smart move artistically because the dialogue communicated more effectively with the audience than narration would. And it also relieved Pathiel from the full burden of so much language.

One of the things that is so moving about the *Undesirable Elements* process is that the people whose story it's about give voice to their own stories. Watching Ping listen to all of those voices and then tease-out how to present the stories so well, with the fewest number of words, it's magic. It's phenomenal to watch that process happen. Can you tell I'm a big fan?

What was it like producing *Secret Histories: Seattle Youth?*

It was very clear to me when I saw the show in New York how it worked. There's always going to be a semi-circle of chairs facing the audience and maybe rock salt covering the floor, slides projected onto the back wall, lights.

When we zeroed in on Seattle youth as our subject, Ping said, "Let's see if we can work with a broad range of Seattle youth." We did a lot of groundwork before Ping even landed in Seattle. We reached out to any organization that worked with youth in Seattle and told them that we wanted to reach kids who wanted to tell their stories. If you're interested in being a human being on this planet there's no end to the *Undesirable Elements* question.

Ping brings a lot of himself into the room. To work with the kids who were in *Seattle Youth*, you have to establish trust. The kids knew me; they met Ping, and I told them how I saw Ping tell his story in the performance in New York. That made a big difference to them. I told them there are no wrong answers here; we want to hear from them.

Ping has this energy that makes it seem as if he's got all the time in the world for you. Sara has it, too. Some of the kids didn't speak English so well and were halting. Never was there a rushed moment in the room. It was as if time would stop and Ping had all the time in the world to listen to that story. While keeping track of different threads of the story, Ping would pick up a thread and bring it back. For instance, "Pathiel, you mentioned that the attackers would come through the villages and tie you up. Is that where you got the scars on your forehead from?" And Pathiel went back to something he had said an hour before.

I was gobstopped by Ping. He wasn't even taking notes. He would always keep complete eye contact with the kids; he built complete trust. Collaborating with him was tremendous. Listening to him and Sara talk after the interviews—this was early in Sara's experience and Ping was giving Sara tremendous trust, with her writing out whole chunks—was magnificent to watch. I've been in interview situations with teenagers before, but this was unique.

What was the impact of *Secret Histories: Seattle Youth?*

We set out wanting to tell authentic youth stories from Seattle and that was absolutely achieved, and the impact that it had on the kids who got to see the piece was far beyond what we had imagined. The student audiences—and this is why we did the show, for the student audience—were blown away.

One of the students, Evin, was our youngest in the group. One of the student matinees was a sold-out show to his high school. He's a pretty popular kid. It was striking to see, in the talk-back after the show: people saying, "I didn't know that about you." It was something to hear: that people who had known him for a long time, kids who, for all intents and purposes, see themselves as Evin's close friends, didn't know what he'd been through.

When Abdi-Karim talked about the morning he was taken away from his parents in a refugee camp in Somalia, kids, who thought the worst thing that happened to them that morning was their parents taking away their cell phones, saw and experienced difference. And that was why we did the show.

The response from most of the kids was complete shock. And then they'd start saying, "Everyone has to see this." It was amazing to see kids waking up, realizing that there are many more layers to each of us—it was the art of storytelling that did that.

It reminded me of the true healing power of theater. The five kids who told their stories and I have stayed in touch. It's been wonderful to see them grow, to see them grow more confident. Stephanie was struggling with mental health issues. She's now an advocate in the community, and she talks about how working with Ping confirmed for her the path she was on.

Pathiel was never reunited with his family, and he now refers to the Seattle Rep as his family. I always tell Pathiel when I'm going to talk to Ping. He says, "Please tell them that I love them, that they're my family." He was very struck that telling a story can help someone else through a tough time. People often said in post-show discussions, "I can't believe what you've been through, you are so brave, you've inspired, me." He was just bearing witness and telling his story. It could help someone else and that was healing for him.

Undesirable Elements takes the mirror up to your heart and says, "Here it is, have a look; that's what's going on inside."

FRANCES KAO is the Public Program Manager at Seattle Repertory Theatre.

SOULA ANTONIOU AND ELENA WIDDER

Commissioners and Producing Partners, VSA, *Inside/Out . . .
voices from the disability community*

VA: How did you first encounter *Undesirable Elements*?

EW: We had been approached by Ping and Bruce [Allardice, managing director of Ping Chong + Company] through VSA arts of New Mexico. I had heard about Ping's work; they had done a piece through our affiliate in New Mexico. Ping came to us interested in doing an *Undesirable Elements* about disability culture, delving into the subject of disability. In terms of *Undesirable Elements*, he is interested in the point of view of the other and those outside of mainstream culture. This was a story that needed to be shown.

SA: We were at a point in our program development where we were looking for projects to commission. At the time, I was on travel and Elena was on travel, so we asked two staff people in New York to see the piece Ping Chong was doing at the time, *Undesirable Elements/Asian America.*

Before we sat down with Ping and Bruce, we weren't sure that disability would resonate in this format. We wanted to be sure that Ping and Bruce felt they could capture disability as well as they had other more specific communities. The range of disabilities and the breadth of disability—for instance, someone with a newly acquired disability has a different experience from someone born with a disability.

195

We wanted to be true to the disability story and to the *Undesirable Elements* project and serve both organizations well. We worked very hard and successfully to convey our mission and values to Ping and Sara while they were developing the piece.

Both VSA and Ping Chong + Company remained flexible about how we worked. The most important part was the casting. We had certain parameters that we told Ping and Sara about. We helped them identify artists with disabilities in the New York community. We discussed the importance of the performers being willing and honest in telling their stories to an audience and the need for people who were comfortable performing. We discussed political issues that VSA is aware of as well as Ping and Sara's needs. I respected the application questionnaire and interview process.

From my perspective, the vision perspective, the forty-thousand-foot view, I wanted the piece to capture the disability experience with integrity and in an authentic way. I was confident that the art would be excellent, that the theater piece would be excellent, but I really wanted it to be authentic, to capture the range of disability experience. If we could get an audience to sit down and hear the oral history of that experience, I wanted them to walk away knowing something that they didn't know when they walked into the theater. I wanted a change to happen, I wanted a perspective shift.

The single issue facing people with disability is the disability stigma and the perception about what you can't do. If disability was captured authentically, I was confident that people's perceptions would change. That these seven experiences would demonstrate that disability matters and that there's something about disability that all of us can learn from; that there's a place for this in our society.

EW: The audience related to these people as humanized people with disability. They came away feeling that these people were human beings, that they were approachable—they shared something with them. So many people said, "I loved so and so's story because it reminded me of something in my own life."

It was great to see these performers after the show being treated like rock stars. Everyone wanted to get to know them because they had such interesting stories.

SA: It really was executed quite brilliantly. It dispelled the myths of disability in a very humane way. And a very funny way.

EW: People think disability is very serious, and it was great to show the humor.

SA: Blair, who uses a wheelchair, tells a story about sex—everybody wonders about it; everyone's afraid to ask, but she's up front about it. That commonality—the show created that bridge for people. It dispelled the myths, the fear, the inability to pursue an honest answer. You have to put yourself out there to ask the question. And the show asked a lot of important questions in order to capture the disability experience.

What was the impact of *Inside/Out* on the performers?

SA: The experience of being in the show was very powerful for all the performers. The number one experience was the bonding they found in learning about each other, hearing each other's stories, and saying very personal things—to each other at first, and then to a public audience. Several of them had family members who had never heard some of their stories before. Some of them were coming out about their feelings for the first time. The family members were thrilled to have their loved one's stories told and accepted. To hear the audience acceptance was amazing.

The cast members formed a very strong bond. In a radio interview about the show, they could fill in where interviewer Bob Edwards had questions about a cast member who wasn't there. They had really listened to each other, and the interplay between them onstage was real. They heard each other; they felt each other. Something happened that was above and beyond these seven people.

EW: It was also important that the cast was intergenerational. In the end, the youngest was twenty-three and the oldest was sixty.

SA: During the development of the piece, Christopher, the youngest performer in the show, used the term "post-ADA experience" to express how different life is since the Americans with Disabilities Act became law in 1990. In the initial casting we didn't have that, and we said we have to have someone in their early twenties in order to hear an authentic post-ADA experience. Ping and Bruce said we hear you—that was the beauty of the collaboration, we really respected each other's needs.

Also interesting was Vivian's story. She was the oldest member of the cast but had also come to disability latest in life. The beauty of Sara and Ping's writing is the suspense: What is Vivian's story? The audience was on the edge of their seats wanting to know what's going to happen.

197

Vivian provided a commonality that we will all experience. It was difficult to determine what her disability was at first, because she lost her vision well into adulthood. In the show she stressed that most of us in the baby boom generation will experience disability in our lifetime. That's an important message.

Josh talking about how his life was affected by his mother's disability. The story of living with someone with a disability, is another aspect of life with disability that people could relate to.

It was a phenomenal collaboration. It was easy; philosophically everybody was on the same page, everybody was committed to the artistic integrity of the piece. We had the world premiere at the Kennedy Center in Washington, D.C., and then we felt it had to be seen by a wider audience, so we moved it to New York. In my dream world we could take the piece throughout the country. It carries an important message for people to hear.

EW: The bottom line is, it was entertaining. People think a piece about disability will be humorless, serious.

SA: The piece had a lot of charm to it. I don't think people expected to be charmed by it.

EW: The cast was open and able to laugh at themselves which gave the audience permission to laugh with them, instead of at them. Matthew, for instance, has Moebius syndrome, and his face can't move, which can put off strangers. Once the audience got to know his personality through his performance, they adored him. His timing and his sense of humor were terrific.

SA: That spoke to Ping and Sara and Bruce's ability to edit and to make the piece fresh, keeping it succinct so that the audience wanted more when the piece was over. The Actor's Equity contract we had with the Kennedy Center required that it be ninety minutes or less. They had to keep tightening, tightening and tightening. They had to do a lot of judicious cutting.

EW: You could see how much they had to edit down. The initial interviews were very long. The editing job was masterful.

Did *Inside/Out* have the impact you had hoped for?

SA: The message is that disability matters, disability is important, disability is beautiful, disability is powerful. I wanted people to have that experience with disability and this piece did it in a thousand different ways.

I wanted the disability voices to be heard. One of the reasons that we've been commissioning new work is that we realize the disability experience has not been captured in the art world. Maybe the experience of an artist with a disability has been captured, but the disability experience has not been captured. This was the first oral history theater project on disability, and to work with the best people who do that—Ping Chong + Company—was important. We wanted it in the mainstream art community because we don't want "separate but equal." How are we going to change perceptions about disability if we aren't getting artistic institutions to think about disability holistically, which is what I hope this piece did.

It even made the disability community think about ourselves. I was talking to an old friend of mine who's been in the disability community for twenty years. I said, "I'm curious about what you, someone who has worked on disability issues, thinks." He said, "Oh my god, I realized I haven't been thinking about the young generation. I love the phrase 'post-ADA.' I'm going to have to think more about how we work with young people." He realized that people born after the Americans with Disabilities Act had different expectations than older members of the disability community. The power of the piece was that, because it was authentic and captured the range and breadth of disability, everybody can walk away with something new.

EW: People who had lived with disability their whole lives had a different take from people who hadn't heard these stories before. People for whom this was new, it was the most powerful thing they'd ever seen. You have to change people's perceptions and stereotypes, but you don't want to shove it down their throats. Make it entertaining and, before you know it, they walk out a changed person. We don't want to preach or lecture.

SA: We really wanted to reach a mainstream audience. The whole point is to create work that is through the lens of disability but speaks to the mainstream.

There's been a big impact from *Inside/Out* on a couple of different levels. Doing the piece demonstrated that there is a place for us in the theater community, and there is a place for us to get our message out in a creative and appropriate way. It made me want to do an even bigger piece that is global in nature. I want to do a global *Inside/Out* now. If we can capture the experience across the world, that would be great.

SOULA ANTONIOU is an accomplished leader with more than two decades of experience in the not-for-profit and public sectors. She served for eight years as President of VSA, the international organization on arts and disability, an affiliate of The John F. Kennedy Center for the Performing Arts. Under her leadership, new affiliates were launched throughout the U.S. and in fifty-one countries and participation in VSA's programs grew to more than seven million people. Ms. Antoniou produced award-winning international events, and commissioned a series of inclusive, accessible and high-profile productions such as *Inside/Out*.

ELENA WIDDER is a Washington, D.C., arts administrator whose most recent position was as Vice President for Public Awareness at VSA. She is currently a consultant to local and national arts organizations, as well as an independent theater producer.

LEYLA MODIRZADEH

Collaborator and Performer, *Undesirable Elements/Seattle* and *Undesirable Elements Anniversary Productions*; Co-writer and Director, *Secret Histories: Journeys Abroad, Journeys Within* (2004 and 2005); Creator, *Secret Histories: Oxford*

VA: How did you first encounter Undesirable Elements?

LM: I was cast in *Undesirable Elements/Seattle* in 1995. Tim Bond, artistic director of the Group Theatre said, "We have this renowned director coming out, Ping Chong." I interviewed with Ping and I loved him. He was such a funny guy. Over the years I've been in several *Undesirable Elements*—I've written, directed and created my own piece in the series.

Tell us about the *Secret Histories: Oxford* that you created.

Just this morning I got a call from a woman who was in the show in Mississippi. The project affected her so much that she wants me to come back to Mississippi and do another. Her church wants to do one. I had to help her with her lines for hours every Saturday at her farm. She grew up picking cotton and hadn't been able to learn to read very well; she had had this life—fourteen kids lived in two rooms, rural Mississippi poverty.

I moved to a small town in Mississippi because my husband was going to graduate school there, and I knew the area had a strong regional identity. I thought it would lend itself to an interesting *Secret History*. I called Ping and Sara [Zatz, project director of the *Undesirable Elements* series] and said, "Would you back me if I do an *Undesirable Elements* down here?" And they were great and said, "Sure, sure."

I found people to include. I did extensive interviews and transcribed them. I loved the vernacular, so I transcribed the interviews myself, which took hours, but I got the melody of their language: someone from the Delta, someone who had recently arrived from Japan. Then I kept whittling down to the strongest stories. I sent them to Ping and Sara and they gave me feedback and I kept revising and getting more feedback. I had fourteen drafts.

The space we performed in wasn't really a theater, and I didn't have any technical support. It was such a shoestring show—I got my husband to do the sound. A music store donated the music stands. Then it opened, and it was a big deal in the community.

Some older white women who had been in the community forever and seen everything—they'd seen segregation; they'd seen the integration of Old Miss—they came up to me after the show in tears and said, "Did you make this? We just want to thank you. We've been waiting for someone to tell these stories. Thank you so much."

It meant so much to Annie Hollowell who got to tell her own story in the show. She told the story of her breast cancer and of her husband coming in and seeing her in the bath after her mastectomy and jumping back. So brave, so powerful. Annie Hallowell's family didn't know everything she told, but onstage she was able to tell them. She brought her whole church.

We had a man who was half Mexican and gay. Annie Hollowell didn't think she'd ever met a gay person, and at first she didn't want to sit next to him or talk to him. But she got to know him and to like him and would throw her arms around him by the end.

At the end of the Mississippi show there was not a dry eye in the house, everybody cried. The show is so cathartic for the community. In the safety of a darkened theater you can let yourself think about things that are usually too charged. You can really have a moment of feeling and understanding.

It's a small community, but I had a little journal outside that people could write in. People wrote beautiful things about what it was like to watch it. The chair of the University of Mississippi theater department told me it was the most moving theater she had ever seen. On the basis of that show, she hired me to teach. She included a chapter about the show in her book *Enacting History*.

That show was done by nothing other than me and my time, and Sara and Ping and Bruce [Allardice, Ping Chong + Company's managing director] giving me feedback by email and phone—yet it was a deep experience for a lot of people, and it had a huge impact in that community. And it keeps going. Annie Hollowell keeps calling. I really fell in love with Mississippi.

Undesirable Elements is a great format. Ping came up with something pretty genius. It's just deceptively simple. It can be really amazing artistically.

Through the lens of *Undesirable Elements* you can contemplate the personal specifics and universal truths for any group. Everyone has histories and love and loss and issues with their parents. The show really humanizes everybody.

LEYLA MODIRZADEH acts, writes and directs for theater and film. Her many stage credits include her own original work and *Undesirable Elements* projects in Seattle, New York and Mississippi.

VICTORIA ABRASH is a dramaturg and arts programming consultant. She is the Program Director for the National Performing Arts Convention and teaches theater at Eugene Lang College of the New School and NYU's Playwrights Horizons Theater School. She collaborated with Ping Chong on an early music adaptation of *Edda: Viking Tales of Lust and Revenge*, which was presented at the 2001 Lincoln Center Theater Festival. Her interview with Ping Chong is included in the anthology of his plays *The East-West Quartet*.

Methodology

Methodology: An Overview

By Sara Zatz

Associate Director of Ping Chong + Company /
Project Director of the *Undesirable Elements* series

INTRODUCTION AND IMPACT

Undesirable Elements is an ongoing series of community-specific interview-based theater works that examine the real lives of people who in some way are living as "outsiders" in their communities. *Undesirable Elements* is not a traditional play or documentary-theater project performed by actors. Instead, it is presented as a chamber piece of storytelling. Or, as Ping Chong says, *Undesirable Elements* is "a seated opera for the spoken word."

Undesirable Elements exists as an open framework that can be brought to any community, and be tailored to suit the needs and issues facing that community. Each production is made with a local host organization—a theater, museum, university, arts center, or community organization—with local participants testifying to their real lives and experiences. The development process includes an extended community residency, during which Ping Chong, myself, and/or other artistic collaborators conduct intensive interviews with potential participants, getting to know the issues and concerns facing the individuals and the community as a whole.

These interviews, adapted and occasionally theatricalized, form the basis of the script that weaves participants' individual experiences together in a chronological narrative, touching on both political and personal experiences. The script is always performed by the interviewees themselves, and they retain a final right of review and approval. Most have never before spoken publicly about their life experiences; many have never before performed on stage.

Typically, as many as twenty-five individuals may be interviewed for a final group of five to eight participants. We seek a group that will represent a diversity of voices and experiences, and speak openly and honesty about struggles of identity, culture and otherness within different communities.

The resulting production is a chamber piece of personal testimonies by the performers, addressing the recent history of the twentieth and twenty-first centuries, and the collisions of peoples and cultures in the modern world.

Like a sonnet, each work in the series retains a standard structure and form, with creative and topical variations from production to production. In the early years of the series, the participants shared nothing in common other than their geographic residency in the specific city of the work. In recent years, there has been a marked increase in requests for productions as communities around the country struggle with complex issues of difference, tolerance and American identity. As such, the project has evolved and its thematic nature has expanded. Early productions focused more on issues of immigration and national or cultural identity. Recent productions have explored themes as wide ranging as disability, Native American identity, or the experience of child sexual abuse.

Undesirable Elements projects are structured to have three levels of impact, all of which foster greater understanding between individuals and lager communities. On the most intimate level, an *Undesirable Elements* production creates an environment where five to eight individuals from different cultural, generational and social backgrounds, who may never otherwise have met each other, share their most personal life experiences and form intimate and enduring connections during the production process.

On the second level, these disparate performers bring their stories to a diverse audience and share them in a theatrical setting that challenges the viewers' expectations. It is an opportunity for theaters to intentionally engage with their broader community, particularly underserved audiences. Traditionally, *Undesirable Elements* has had two types of audiences—those who are only used to seeing people similar to themselves on stage, and those who almost never have the experience of seeing people similar to themselves on stage. When these two groups come together to experience an *Undesirable Elements*, they form a community on that performance night, experiencing a common exchange with the performers and with each other.

The third, and broadest, level of exchange is the cumulative long-term impact of the previous two components, as the original participants and audience members bring their experiences out to their own communities, thereby broadening the dialogue and understanding generated by the theatrical experience.

THE TOOLS AND THE PROCESS

After two decades of creating the *Undesirable Elements* series, we have been able to streamline the basic process, at least for the beginning stages of the work, which has helped with recruiting and forming the performance groups, simplifying the interview process and creating the scripts.

Because Ping Chong + Company is usually based outside of the host community, the partner organization is primarily responsible for community outreach. Prior to our arrival for the residency, they will begin the recruitment process. The primary requirements are willingness to speak openly about personal experiences, to share space with others whose views and experiences may differ vastly from one's own, and the availability to commit to three weeks of rehearsals and a set number of performances. No prior performance experience is required, and individuals are assured that they will not need to memorize the script. Potential participants are recruited through, listservs, ads in local papers, fliers in community centers, etc. We encourage our partner organizations to "look in their own backyard." As a result, the attendant at the theater's parking garage, or the employee at the deli across the street might easily become part of the show. All you need to do is ask.

Those interested in participating complete a preliminary interview packet, which includes questions about their personal and family background, culture and traditions, and questions that may be related to the overall theme of the show.

The interview packet was created in 2002 to allow us to have a better overview of the participant pool in advance of the initial interviews. The packet was designed based on certain interview questions that Ping always asked. For example: "Are there any unusual stories about the day you were born?" "Have you felt like an outsider in your own community?" "Where is home for you?"

From these packets, a preliminary group is selected for interviews. Initial interviews last approximately two hours, with the artistic team completing two to three interviews per day for up to two weeks. Interviews can be deeply personal (we always tell the host organization to provide tissues). Secondary interviews of an additional one to two hours are conducted with individuals who are chosen to be in the production.

Once the cast has been confirmed, the scripting process begins. The script is developed from the interview materials, the application packet and additional historical research. The lead artist (Ping Chong, myself or another collaborator) typically writes a chronological sequence of dated entries for each participant, which are only woven together later, after each individual's arc is completed. Each production script also contains a number of "standard" sections: The Introductions, The Name Game, Personal and Historical Entries, What Do You Think Of, Songs/Poems, and "Out"roductions, although even these have evolved over the years. Clapping is a rhythmic trope that exists in all productions, with single or double claps punctuating significant entries and driving the momentum forward, and sequences of five or ten claps delineating different sections.

Over the course of the scripting process (which takes place back in New York), we may contact the cast members by phone or email to ask follow-up questions, clarify details or check on a particularly sensitive entry. Typically, the cast members only see the script, and the way their stories have been represented, on the first day of rehearsal, at which point they see it in context with the stories of their fellow performers.

The first two to three rehearsals are dedicated to script revisions. The cast members have the opportunity to request revisions based on historical accuracy, accuracy of voice/tone or privacy. The script will continue to evolve over the course of the rehearsal process, with entries cut or added by the artistic team, but a deadline is set for the cast to submit final changes. In twenty years of productions, no committed cast member has ever left the project as a result of discomfort with their representation in the script. It is a deeply collaborative process, one that requires the establishment of significant trust, and constantly seeks to balance the artistic vision with the need to honor the authentic voices and stories of the participants.

A sample participant questionnaire and impact essay by Matthew S. Joffe, who participated in *Inside/Out . . . voices from the disability community*, follows.

Staging a Comeback

By Matthew S. Joffe

There I was, in a rehabilitation center. In November 2007, I fell and fractured my leg in three places. My Moebius thwarted any hopes of me using crutches and going home and healing. Fast forward and it is now late January 2008 and I am still there. A phone call and e-mail proved to be the lifeline I was seeking. There was an opportunity to be part of a new theater production about disabilities starring people with disabilities. Ironically, the announcement came to me through LaGuardia Community College/CUNY, where I work. I had heard the name Ping Chong, but I knew nothing of his work. After perusing the application, I decided this was the carrot I had been looking for. This play would be the prize for me to walk after nearly three months of enforced bench-warming.

Wow! I never saw questions like these before: "What was the weather like the day you were born?" "What is your earliest memory?" Later I found out that it was from these types of queries and the interviews that followed that the script of *Inside/Out . . . voices from the disability community* was created. I had acted twice before with The Inner Faces Players, but that was different. For the first time I had to audition for the role that would turn out to be myself.

The real excitement associated with this project was that we would give the world premiere at The John F. Kennedy Center for the Performing Arts in Washington, D.C. I would join Actors' Equity and get paid to do what I love—ACT!

Once accepted, I was on cloud nine. I could hardly believe my luck. Rehearsals were being held at LaGuardia Community College, in the actual building where I work, so it couldn't be more convenient. The play's first performance, an open rehearsal, would be Friday, June 13th. Good thing I am not superstitious! I began to worry that rehearsals, beginning May 18th, would be too little too late. It was then that I learned we would be engaged in a special form of acting. We would be sitting on stage at reading stations. No memorizing would be required, but the need for focus, tempo and rhythm was ever present.

The cast, representing a myriad of disabilities, was terrific. We soon felt the sense of family, which made it easier to step in to characters in their stories on stage. I am a music lover (read fanatic) and Ping's choices, Norwegian incantations and Polish orchestral music, were fascinating. I found myself unable to rid them from my mind, which made sleeping difficult.

Ping, Sara, Courtney, all of the staff, were incredibly warm and sensitive. They were eager to learn about us and our disabilities. The writing reflected an uncanny talent for nailing our emotions on the head. I also acted as a consultant on disability, since that is one of my primary functions in my job. The play tells the stories of seven people whose lives have been affected by disability. It chronicles societal awareness and action, as well as documents the trials and triumphs that we have experienced in our lives. In my story, I tell the audience what Moebius is and how it has impacted on my life.

As the performances grew near, I realized that one of the benefits I get from performing is what I refer to as "balancing the books." Each time I go on stage I am putting a plus entry into the column where a negative experience once stood. I bare my soul on stage without the fear I sometimes have walking the streets amidst the stares and jeers that often surface.

Performing for friends, and especially colleagues, allowed me to share aspects of my life that normally remain hidden. It was a bit scary, but you cannot bond with others if you hold back. Taking risks has it rewards. I surprised myself with how emotional I became with my own story. Lines alternatively stifled me with their primal content or shot out of me as a declaration to the world that I will survive and conquer!

An unforeseen moment came when the then Vice President of my division surprised me, driving to opening night at the Kennedy Center. His subsequent e-mail to the college community not only celebrated me and the production, it triggered a stream of comments from my colleagues about the performance *and* my valuable role in the work I do at the college. I was truly humbled by the responses and the knowledge that I make a difference in other peoples' lives.

MATTHEW S. JOFFE is Senior Director, Office for Student Guidance and Disabled Students Programs, at LaGuardia Community College/CUNY. He has more than thirty years' experience as an educational therapist and psychotherapist. In addition, he holds certificates in family and divorce mediation, and chemical-dependency counseling. He maintains a private practice in New York City. In addition to *Inside/Out*, his performing experience includes having co-written and performed in two original plays in New York City. He is a published poet and has appeared in several international documentaries. An avid music lover and collector, his tastes range from classical and world music to the blues and cabaret. He is a constant audience member at the theater and enjoys tasting foods from around the world. He is currently Vice President of the Moebius Syndrome Foundation, USA, and is passionately devoted to educating the world about people with differences.

A version of this essay was first published by the Moebius Syndrome Foundation, *Moebius Syndrome News*, Volume XVII, Issue II, Summer 2008, pp. 10–11.

Matthew S. Joffe: Participant Information Background Form (2008)

PING CHONG + COMPANY

VSA: Theater Project on Disability Experience

Please answer these questions to the best of your knowledge. Do not worry if you do not know an answer; just write that you do not know.

You may ask someone to help you fill out the forms or call the office and ask to dictate, if necessary.

Please answer as specifically as possible. The project is based on your stories and memories and we want to convey as much detail as possible. Use as much space as necessary (but do not feel you need to write a novel!).

If you feel a question is not relevant to your experience, you may skip it or modify it to reflect your experience.

What is your full name? If different from your birth name, please list your current name and your name at birth. Do you have a separate traditional/cultural name?

Matthew Seth Joffe.

What is your current profession?

Director, Office for Students with Disabilities, LaGuardia Community College/CUNY; Educational Therapist and Psychotherapist in private practice.

Where and when were you born (date, year, city, country)?

June 15, 1953, New York City, USA.

What time of day were you born and what season/time of year was it? (rainy season, winter, at the full moon, etc.)

10:24 A.M., ending of spring, fair and pleasant, temperature range min. 57 to max. 76.

How much did you weigh at birth?

8 lbs. 6 oz.

Did anyone ever tell you any stories of the day you were born (you were born during a blizzard, in a taxi, on your mother's birthday, etc.)?

N/A.

Does your name have any special meaning, and were you named for anyone?

I was named for my Uncle Morris, on my mother's side, who was shot down during WWII. My mother liked the name because it was musical sounding.

How many brothers and sisters do you have? What is your place in the birth order?

I have one sister, seven years younger.

What is your earliest memory?

My earliest memory is at six months. My paternal grandmother is peering over my crib and playing with the mobile.

What language did you speak growing up? What language(s) do you speak at home now?

I spoke English at home. The doctors advised my parents not to raise me bilingual (Yiddish) due to my disability. I currently speak English at home. To this day, I am sorry I did not learn Yiddish.

What are/were your parents' names? What is/was their profession?

Samuel Joffe—CPA; Systems Financial Control Manager (Comptroller); Florence Joffe—Executive Secretary.

Do you know your grandparents' names and professions? If so, please write below. Also note if you knew your grandparents while growing up.

Jacob Epstein—Carpenter.
Sadie Epstein—Homemaker.
Alma Joffe—Retail (Sales) and Bookkeeping.
Samuel Joffe—Owned a Haberdashery Store.

Do you know how your parents met? Are there any stories about their courtship or wedding?

My parents met while working in an accounting firm in NYC. They kept it a secret at work for two years because the policy at the time was that employees could not date each other. They never left the office together and never dated in the vicinity of the office. My mom had to seek permission from her unsuspecting boss to announce her engagement.

Do you know how your grandparents met? Are there any stories about their courtship or wedding?

My maternal grandparents were born in the USSR. Born in two different cities, my grandfather boarded at my grandmother's house when he was an apprentice carpenter. When he arrived he said to himself: "This is a real Krasotka (красотка)—("beauty")—and I am going to marry her."

My paternal grandparents were married through a matchmaker. He was killed in a robbery at work before my father was born. As the custom in Judaism, she married his brother who raised my father.

Please share any unique or unusual stories about your family's history.

My maternal grandmother came with three daughters on a Russian ship as stowaways. While hiding on the ship in an empty room, someone entered the room seeking sex. She talked herself out of the situation, claiming that her screams would wake her children and he would be discharged from the navy.

My father and uncle had to share a suit while attending CUNY. Consequently, they never scheduled classes on the same day throughout their college years.

If not born in NYC, how long have you lived in New York, and what brought you to New York?

I was born in NYC, but raised in Forest Hills, Queens, to age four and then Plainview, Long Island. I went to undergraduate school in Pennsylvania and returned to NYC to go to graduate school in 1975 and I have lived here ever since.

Was there a person in your life who had a profound influence on shaping the person you are today? If so, please give an example of how he/she influenced you.

One of the people who had a significant influence on me was a college professor of psychology, Dr. Josef Brožek. I was fortunate enough to have had him as my "mentor" for the last two years of undergraduate study. I use the term mentor in the English sense, that is, he was my tutor, in all ways educationally and personally. He redefined what education was for me. Through individual attention, I learned about collaborating with others, public speaking and being challenged educationally to think independently and with integrity. He exposed me to many opportunities including writing and publishing and through evening soirees, a breadth of intellectual and cultural situations. He also taught me what it means to give back to someone by transmitting your own knowledge and experience. All of these qualities have helped to shape my commitment and philosophy about teaching and counseling others.

Have you faced issues of identity? How do you currently identify yourself?

I have struggled to understand and embrace what it means to be masculine and have a physical disability. I also grappled with my role as a disabled man, often thinking that I had to "make it" in a nondisabled world. Now, I consider myself as a man with a disability. My disability no longer defines me and I no longer split the world into disabled and nondisabled. I continue to integrate my disability into the work that I do professionally and personally.

What are some assumptions that people make about you?

I have Moebius Syndrome, a rare craniofacial and neurological disorder. People have assumed that I cannot hear and that I am mentally retarded. On a deeper level, people have often not thought of me as a sexual being. They also seem surprised by the fact that I live alone and take care of myself.

Do you have memories of feeling different in your culture of origin and/or current community? Please give an example.

I have, for a long time, thought that there is a type of caste system in our society. Some disabilities are more accepted than others, such as blindness, polio and deafness. My facial disability, for example, often fosters stares and blank looks from people, as if they are trying to process what they are seeing. Without a traditional or recognizable frame of reference (that is, wheelchair or missing limb), they are hard pressed to have a clear understanding of my disability.

Once, as a college freshman, I was home for the summer and accompanied my mother and sister to the community pool to get our season passes. Unable to find a parking space, my mom asked me to pick them up. At the window, the woman, who watched me grow up at the pool, repeatedly asked where my mother was. I kept telling her that she was circling the parking lot. She refused to let go of the passes until I said, "Lady, I have a double major and speak two languages. What is your problem?" Only then did she give me the passes and I returned to the car. Clearly, looks can be deceiving!

Have you experienced direct or indirect discrimination/prejudice? Please give an example.

One that was life changing for me occurred in eighth grade. After having lunch with a friend, we left the cafeteria at opposite ends. He was teased and jumped in the hallway by three other boys. He was sent to the assistant principal. When I arrived he looked dejected and worried. I said that I would speak to the assistant principal on his behalf. "I will be your mouthpiece, your Perry Mason." I went into his office and said that while I do not condone fighting, I did not feel that it was fair for my friend to be punished (suspended) just because he chose me as his friend. I was praised for my loyalty, and he promised that he would not suspend my friend. I left not only feeling that I could stand up for myself and others, but that I was also a survivor.

Have you witnessed discrimination/prejudice within your own community toward others? Please give an example.

As a child in school, I was friends with someone who was very bright who had emotional problems. One link, in my mind, was our lack of prowess and skill in gym. Once, during a swimming session, the lifeguard, who was also our teacher, publicly teased him, just like the kids did. I remember being thoroughly disgusted with his behavior, especially because he was a teacher and supposed to be a role model. I glared at him, never having any respect for him again.

Do you identify as a member of the disability community?

Yes I do, as an advocate for people with disabilities.

What are some of the major issues/concerns that you see as currently pressing within your community?

Deemphasizing the value of superficial beauty in media and our society; employment opportunities with commensurate wages; balancing the power and efficiency of the ADA [Americans with Disabilities Act]; accessibility to community venues and businesses; adequate transportation alternatives; visibility in restaurants where people are seated out of sight.

If you work in the creative arts, how has your personal background informed your artistic work (if it has)?

I do not work professionally in the creative arts field, however, I have worked (acted and written) in several plays and documentaries on disability-related themes.

What do you like about living in New York?

I love the energy of New York—the vibrancy that sets it apart from other cities. I also thrive on the multicultural fabric of the city—the languages, the food and the cultural arts. I also value the freedom and independence that I can have living here.

What do you dislike about living in New York?

I miss being able to go to the countryside without effort (I cannot drive). I also miss having a house where I could I surround myself in its vast spaces and have an enclosed yard filled with dogs.

Where is home for you? If not NYC, what do you miss about your home?

I live in midtown New York on the east side. I do not miss Long Island, where I was raised, because I was dependent on my parents to go anywhere and do anything. I also did not like the predominant white population (I would have preferred diversity), and the absence of other children with disabilities.

How did you hear about this project, and why do you want to participate?

As an employee of LaGuardia Community College and as Director of the Office for Students with Disabilities I was apprised of this project while on temporary medical leave. I am interested in this project for several reasons. First, as both an educator and individual with a disability, I strongly believe that it is critical to raise the level of understanding and awareness in our society. Second, as a member of the Inner Faces Players, which is also a support group, I have co-written and performed in two original theater pieces about living with craniofacial differences that were performed Off-Off-Broadway. Third, having been involved in several documentaries, I am keenly aware of the power that the creative arts can have on the public.

Are there any other details about yourself that you wish to share?

I have struggled to see myself as others perceived me. I was uncertain of how I would handle the responsibility of being a role model. I was too focused on a world I had created, reflecting my own uneasiness with my own disability. Now, I embrace my disability proudly. I have come full circle: instead of running from the eyes cast upon me, I look them straight in the eye. Only then can true acceptance, on both sides, be achieved.

Production/Partner History

Undesirable Elements / 1992–2012

Production/Partner History

Undesirable Elements 1992–2012

1992

UNDESIRABLE ELEMENTS
(Original Production)
PARTNER/VENUE: Artists Space, New York, New York

1993

CLEVELAND
PARTNER: Performance Arts Festival, Cleveland, Ohio
TOURING: Kent State University, Kent, Ohio

NEW YORK CITY
TOURING: SUNY—Stony Brook, New York; West Kortright Center, East Meredith, New York; Art Awareness, Lexington, New York; McCarter Theatre Center (TCG Conference), Princeton, New Jersey; American Museum of Natural History, New York; Henry Street Settlement, New York; Rutgers University, New Brunswick, New Jersey

1994

TWIN CITIES
PARTNER/VENUE: Illusion Theater, Minneapolis
TOURING: Regional, ten years

1995

SEATTLE
PARTNER/VENUE: The Group Theatre, Seattle, Washington

TOKYO (GAIJIN)
PARTNER/VENUE: Tokyo Metropolitan Art Space, Tokyo, Japan

1997

YELLOW SPRINGS
PARTNER/VENUE: Antioch College, Yellow Springs, Ohio

ROTTERDAM
PARTNER/VENUE: Schouwburg Rotterdamse, Rotterdam, Holland
TOURING: Regional
COLLABORATING ARTIST: Dave Schwab

LONG BEACH
PARTNER/VENUE: California State University, Long Beach, California

1998

NEWARK
PARTNER/VENUE: New Jersey Performing Arts Center, Newark, New
Jersey
TOURING: Bloomfield College, Bloomfield, New Jersey

1999

HAMILTON COLLEGE
PARTNER/VENUE: Hamilton College, Clinton, New York

CHICAGO
PARTNER/VENUE: Duncan YMCA Chernin Center for the Arts,
Chicago, Illinois
TOURING: University of Illinois, Chicago, Illinois

EAST HARLEM
PARTNER: Dreamyard
VENUE: Julia de Burgos Cultural Center
COLLABORATING ARTIST: Trinket Monsod

2000

ASIA/PACIFIC/AMERICA
PARTNER: Asian/Pacific/American Studies Program & Institute,
New York University, New York
VENUE: Gene Frankel Theater, New York

WASHINGTON, D.C.
PARTNER/VENUE: Gala Hispanic Theatre, Washington, D.C.
COLLABORATING ARTIST: Michael Rohd

SECRET HISTORY
VENUE: Ohio Theatre, New York
TOURING: Connecticut College, New London, Connecticut

2001

MADISON
PARTNER/VENUE: University of Wisconsin, Madison, Wisconsin

SECRET HISTORIES/CHARLESTON
PARTNER/VENUE: Spoleto Festival USA, Charleston, South Carolina
COLLABORATING ARTIST: Talvin Wilks

ATLANTA
PARTNER: 7 Stages and Youth Arts Connection, a program of Boys &
    Girls Clubs of Metro Atlanta
VENUE: 7 Stages, Atlanta, Georgia
TOURING: Regional
COLLABORATING ARTIST: Talvin Wilks

2002

HANOVER

PARTNER/VENUE: Dartmouth College, Hanover, New Hampshire
COLLABORATING ARTIST: Michael Rohd

UE 92/02

(Anniversary Production)
VENUE: La MaMa E.T.C., New York
TOURING: Lille Capital of Culture Festival, Lille, France, 2003
COLLABORATING ARTIST: Talvin Wilks

CHILDREN OF WAR

Fairfax, Virginia
PRODUCING PARTNER: Center for Multicultural Human Services
VENUE: Theater for the First Amendment, George Mason University
TOURING: Grantmakers in Health Conference, Los Angeles, 2003;
National Conference of Catholic Bishops, Washington, D.C.,
2003; Nathan Cummings Foundation, New York, 2003; Ford
Foundation, New York, 2003; World Bank, Washington, D.C.,
2003; UNHCR's World Refugee Day, Washington, D.C., 2003;
Cuyahoga Community College, Cleveland, Ohio, 2004

2003

BERLIN

PARTNER/VENUE: House of World Cultures, Berlin, Germany
COLLABORATING ARTIST: Michael Rohd

PIONEER VALLEY

PARTNER/VENUE: New WORLD Theatre, Amherst, Massachusetts
COLLABORATING ARTIST: Talvin Wilks

2004

SECRET HISTORIES: SEATTLE YOUTH

PARTNER/VENUE: Seattle Repertory Theatre, Seattle, Washington
COLLABORATING ARTIST: Sara Zatz

SECRET HISTORY: JOURNEYS ABROAD, JOURNEYS WITHIN
PARTNER: Lincoln Center Institute
VENUE: Clark Studio Theater, Lincoln Center, New York
TOURING: New York City schools
COLLABORATING ARTISTS: Leyla Modirzadeh and Sara Zatz

UE 92/04
(Anniversary Production)
VENUE: RomaEuropa Festival, Rome, Italy
COLLABORATING ARTIST: Talvin Wilks

2005

NATIVE VOICES-SECRET HISTORY
PARTNER/VENUE: Lied Center of Kansas, Lawrence, Kansas
COLLABORATING ARTIST: Sara Zatz

TEN YEARS LATER
PARTNER/VENUE: Illusion Theater, Minneapolis, Minnesota
COLLABORATING ARTIST: Sara Zatz

UE 92/05
(Anniversary Production)
VENUE: Colorado Festival of World Theatre, Colorado Springs,
    Colorado
COLLABORATING ARTISTS: Talvin Wilks and Sara Zatz

SECRET HISTORY: JOURNEYS ABROAD, JOURNEYS WITHIN
PARTNER: Lincoln Center Institute
VENUE: Clark Studio Theater, Lincoln Center, New York
COLLABORATING ARTISTS: Leyla Modirzadeh and Sara Zatz

2006

ALBUQUERQUE
PARTNER/VENUE: VSA North Fourth Art Center, Albuquerque, New
    Mexico
COLLABORATING ARTIST: Sara Zatz

2012

CRY FOR PEACE: VOICES FROM THE CONGO

PARTNER: Syracuse University; Syracuse Stage, Syracuse, New York

PREMIERE: Syracuse Stage, Syracuse, New York

WORKSHOP PRODUCTIONS: Syracuse Stage, Syracuse, New York; Beckett Theater, New York; Gonda Theatre, Georgetown University

COLLABORATING ARTISTS: Kyle Bass and Sara Zatz

ONGOING

GLOBAL KIDS

(1998–present)

Partnering with not-for-profit youth leadership program Global Kids and New York City public school students to create annual after-school youth productions since 1998.

VENUES: Global Kids Youth Conference; various public institutions.

COLLABORATING ARTIST: Trinket Monsod

SECRET HISTORIES

(Education Program, 2008–present)

Ping Chong + Company's arts-in-education program. The program provides a professional performance, followed by an artistic residency focused on working with students to develop and relate a personal narrative and present it in theatrical terms. The work promotes understanding and sensitivity to others through students' sharing their stories with their peers.

COLLABORATING ARTIST: Jesca Prudencio

VISUAL ARTS INSTALLATIONS

A FACILITY FOR THE CONTAINMENT AND CHANNELING OF UNDESIRABLE ELEMENTS

Artists Space, New York City, New York, 1992

TESTIMONIAL

TransCulture Exhibition,
Venice Biennale, Venice, Italy, 1995

TESTIMONAIL II

Williams Center for the Arts, Easton, Pennsylvania, 2006

PING CHONG is an internationally acclaimed theater director, playwright, video and installation artist. He is a seminal figure in the interdisciplinary theater community and pioneer in the use of media, puppetry, documentary theater and other experimental forms in theater. Since 1972, he has created more than ninety works for the stage committed to artistic beauty and social justice. In 1975, he formed Ping Chong + Company with a mission to create works of theater and art that explore the intersections of race, culture, history, art, media and technology in the modern world. The company has performed at major festivals and theaters around the world, including The John F. Kennedy Center for the Performing Arts, Lincoln Center Festival, Brooklyn Academy of Music, La MaMa E.T.C., Spoleto USA Festival, Vienna Festival, RomaEuropa Festival, Lille European Capital of Culture, Tokyo International Arts Festival, Singapore Festival of the Arts, and many others. During the past forty years, Mr. Chong has addressed themes and issues, such as the clash of Eastern and Western cultures (*Pojagi*, *After Sorrow*, *Chinoiserie*, *Deshima*), genocide in the Congo (*BLIND NESS*), the impact of war on refugees and children (*Children of War*) and corporate greed in America (*Truth & Beauty*).

In 1992, Mr. Chong created the first work in the *Undesirable Elements* series. Producing partners have included Spoleto USA Festival, Lincoln Center Institute, Seattle Repertory Theatre, Syracuse Stage, the Gala Hispanic Theatre, the Boys and Girls Club of Atlanta, and the YMCA of Chicago. Since 1992, there have been more than forty *Undesirable Elements* projects, exploring such themes as the Native American experience, living with a disability, Asian-American identity, and the experiences of refugees.

Mr. Chong has also worked in both media and visual arts, creating award-winning video and visual arts installations that have been exhibited widely in the United States and abroad, including the 1995 Venice Biennale TransCulture show. He has taught at numerous universities, including Harvard, New York University and many others. His many honors and awards include a Guggenheim Fellowship, four New York Foundation for the Arts Fellowships, two BESSIE Awards and two OBIE Awards, including one for Sustained Achievement in 2000. In 2006, he was named a USA Artist Fellow in recognition of his contributions to American arts and culture.

In 2005, TCG published his first play anthology, *The East-West Quartet*. Other published works include *Kind Ness* (which received the 1998 USA Playwrights Award), *Nuit Blanche*, *Snow*, *Undesirable Elements/New York*, *Gaijin*, *Truth & Beauty*, *Undesirable Elements/Asian America* and *Cocktail*.

SARA ZATZ is the Associate Director of Ping Chong + Company and Project Director of the *Undesirable Elements* series. Affiliated with Ping Chong + Company since 1997, she joined the company full-time in 2002 to coordinate the *Undesirable Elements* series. Working in collaboration with partner organizations, ranging from regional theaters to community-based arts organizations, she has managed the production of nearly two dozen original works in the series, exploring themes such as the experiences of people with disabilities, immigrants and refugees, and disenfranchised youth. She has interviewed hundreds of individuals from all over the world and served as co-author with Ping Chong on numerous productions in the series, including *Undesirable Elements/Asian America*, which was published in the 2008 *New York Theater Review*. In 2011, she wrote and directed *Secret Survivors*, an *Undesirable Elements* production exploring the first-hand experiences of adult survivors of child sexual abuse. Additionally, she has overseen the creation of Ping Chong + Company's in-school arts education program and training institutes to share the methodology of *Undesirable Elements* with other artists and community members. She has also worked with the Henson International Festival of Puppet Theater, the composer Tan Dun and Lincoln Center Festival. She holds an M.Phil in Irish Theatre Studies from Trinity College, Dublin, and a BA from Bryn Mawr College.

TALVIN WILKS is a director, playwright and dramaturg based in New York City. Directorial projects include *On the Way to Timbuktu* by Petronia Paley, *Relativity* by Cassandra Medley, *UDU* by Sekou Sundiata, *No Black Male Show* by Carl Hancock Rux, *The Shaneequa Chronicles* by Stephanie Berry, *The Love Space Demands* by Ntozake Shange and the D.C. premiere of *Anne and Emmet* by Janet Langhart Cohen. He has served as co-director/

co-writer/dramaturg for nine productions in Ping Chong's ongoing series of *Undesirable Elements/Secret Histories*, and dramaturg for five collaborations with the Bebe Miller Company: *Necessary Beauty*; *Going to the Wall*; *Verge*; *Landing/Place*, for which he received a 2006 Bessie Award; and the upcoming premiere of *A History*. He is currently writing a book on black theater: *Testament: 40 Years of Black Theatre History in the Making, 1964–2004*, and curated *The Aunt Ester Cycle*, a theater festival for the inaugural season at the August Wilson Center for African American Culture in Pittsburgh, Pennsylvania.